Old Mother, Little Cat

Old Mother, Little Cat

A Writer's Reflections
on Her Kitten, Her Aged Mother
. . . and Life

Merrill Joan Gerber

LONGSTREET PRESS, INC.
Atlanta, Georgia

Published by
LONGSTREET PRESS, INC.
A subsidiary of Cox Newspapers,
A division of Cox Enterprises, Inc.
2140 Newmarket Parkway
Suite 118
Marietta, GA 30067

Printed in the United States

1st printing 1995

Library of Congress Catalog Card Number: 95-77244

ISBN 1-56352-249-7

Book design by Jill Dible, typesetting by Laura McDonald
Jacket design by Jill Dible
Jacket photograph by James Bozman

For my mother,

JESSIE SORBLUM GERBER,

who was awarded

The Eighth Grade Gold Medal

For Academic Excellence

at Public School 9, New York City

June 1920

Foreword

As I write these words, four years have passed since my mother began her existence in a nursing home. For the last three of those years, she has been paralyzed and connected to a feeding tube. Most recently, for the last several weeks, she has not even been able to sit up in a wheelchair. She is turned every two hours from one side to another and propped in place with pillows. What constitutes variety in her life now has to do with whether she is facing east or west.

"I am *so* tired of being in one place," she told me at our last visit. "What *use* is a life like this?"

Over the years of her illness I had pretty much run out of answers for that question, but on this day (when I arrived to show her the book jacket design for *Old Mother, Little Cat*), a new answer occurred to me suddenly, one I had never given her before.

"Maybe you could think of it this way, Ma—that you are living these difficult years for *me*. Maybe because you have to have this experience (and I am having it, in my way, too), we are both making something valuable from it. *Old Mother, Little Cat* is what came of it. And maybe other nursing home patients and their children who are going through a time like this will read it and learn something from our experience that may help them."

I could see my mother considering this, could see the intensity in her eyes as she pondered this newly drawn perception of her condition. Finally she said, "Maybe that *is* a good way to think about it."

What a magician's trick, I thought, if I could make my mother believe that what she had suffered in the last years was a present to me, a gift, one of the many sacrifices she had fervently and willingly made so that I could move forward in my life. Still, the idea actually appeared to please her. She studied my face, seemed to be pondering what I had suggested.

"Yes, it's true," she said slowly. "You couldn't have written this book without me."

"This book, and everything else I've ever done," I added truthfully.

For just the briefest moment, a smile lit her face.

I taped the book jacket illustration on the wall opposite her bed as she indicated where I should place it among the family photos. She nodded her satisfaction.

When a few moments later the nurse came in with her cart of medications, my mother proudly pointed out the new addition on the wall. The book's existence proclaimed an irrefutable truth: that my mother had lived in the world, that she had given birth to me (the author), and that she felt—at least for this moment—entitled and proud to take credit for all her accomplishments.

I don't know if my inspired interpretation of my mother's plight, should she remember it, will continue to offer any comfort to her at all through the coming painful days or years, but the truth is that writing *Old Mother, Little Cat* has comforted *me* during her long struggle, and for that I am grateful.

— M.J.G.

Merrill Joan Gerber

Old Mother, Little Cat

December 17

On this particular December morning, I am having enough troubles as it is: troubles of the heart that can't be fixed as well as ordinary troubles that can be. Even as I kick an old towel around on the kitchen floor to sop up the leak from the dishwasher, I'm thinking of what I need to take to my mother today at the nursing home: mints, a small pillow for her paralyzed arm, the sharp scissors so I can give her a haircut—*if* the nurses have been able to convince her to sit up in the wheelchair for a while. I'm also making mental lists of the errands I have to run afterward.

In order not to flood the floor, I grab the dripping towel and run with it to the back door. I do this automatically—I wring it out and hang it over the pool wall, I gather up the dry one from yesterday in order to lay it down under the leak. J., my good husband and man of the house, definitely plans to fix this leak, but I don't think he has the faintest idea of what is wrong. Still, he says he's not ready for me to call a plumber. He wants to think about it a little more.

My mind is everywhere at once; I need to do food shopping at the market after I see my mother. My college girls are coming home for the Christmas break in a few days and I'll need lots more grains and vegetables (J. and I haven't quite given up our meat and buttered potatoes diet, though we've improved).

I stand outside near the pool for a moment, watching the water drip from the towel, looking around at the bleak winter view, at the dead leaves on the deck, at the pecans from the tree floating like black beetles in the icy water.

A squadron of crows descends on the lawn, calling out with loud caws for others to join them to forage for newly fallen pecans. In this gray morning hour, the large birds, bent forward over their task, look like black stones on the paltry stretch of winter grass.

And it is then, just then, that I hear the cry. It seems to come almost from the tips of my toes—the saddest, most forlorn moan I have ever heard.

"What is it?" I cry automatically.

But there is only silence. Did I imagine it?

I look around now, alert and aware; I sense nothing but the faint movement of the trees in the chill winter wind (a cold wind, even for California) and the occasional clack of a crow.

I am about to go inside when the sound comes again. It's an urgent sound, as close to a plea as it can be without words. Is it our old cat, Kitty, hurt or trapped? Even as I imagine this, Kitty appears on the pool wall, walking in his slow, majestic way, his great old gray coat thick and fluffed with winter fur. When the cry repeats itself, we both hear it. Kitty freezes and stares at my feet. Nothing is there but patterns on the darkened cement—the splotchy water stains that are dripping from the towel.

"What is it, where are you?" I say again. The cry is vocal now, loud, full of pain, desperate. Then I see something just behind the wire screen that covers a square opening under the house, a crawl space to a place where no one ever goes. Something is pressed against the grids. I kneel down and see a pair of round green eyes looking back at me. They are both like little mouths open in terror.

"Oh my God," I say to Kitty. "It's some kind of creature."

The creature opens its mouth to cry out as if to verify this, and I hear the sound clearly and recognize it for what it is.

The meow of a kitten. Oh no. No, I won't think of it. Absolutely not. I won't consider it. I am done with these matters. I don't have the strength for it. I've done my duty: three children, a dog, dozens of mice, fish, birds, and two cats, one of which (Korky, the Beloved) we buried two years ago in the back yard at a solemn funeral rite. Only old Kitty is left, and when he dies, which J. hopes will be in our lifetime, we can finally travel somewhere without endless arrangements and worries.

The hackles are up on Kitty's back; he wants no new friend, either. Fine. We're in agreement.

Go inside and forget about him. The next time you come out he'll be gone.

Even as I'm thinking this, I'm trying to pull the screen away from its frame, saying, "Shh, shh, don't be afraid, little one, you'll be fine, no one is going to hurt you." (Whose voice could this be? It can't be mine, not when I'm thinking something else entirely!) With a great heave of my arm (I wrench my back doing it), the rusted old screen comes away and the green eyes withdraw and vanish. I get a glimpse of something hopping, bunny-like, away into the dark recesses under the house.

My heart is full. I feel passionate, a long-gone sensation I barely recognize. I'm energized, full of purpose. I rush into the house and get a bowl and fill it with milk. I shake some of Kitty's dry food into a plate. I don't say a word to J., who is reading the paper at the kitchen table. This will have to be a secret between me and Kitty, who has followed me into the house and whose eyes are narrowed as he watches me.

Outside again, I set the food dishes down in the place where I first saw the green eyes, in the hollow dark place under the house, on plain dirt. In the twenty-five years we've lived here, I've never really looked into this hole, into the cavernous darkness there. How could a kitten have gotten underneath, into this inhospitable cave? And why did he stay?

I wait, watching the food bowls, but there is no sound, no motion. Even Kitty, seeing that I have set out food, and having a passion for almost nothing else, does not try to venture there.

I look at him, fat and furred, in his thick gray coat. His enormous paws are like cartoon drawings. He, too, appeared in our lives as if by design on a day at least twelve years ago, now. J. was in the driveway with our daughters, all of them washing the station wagon. The tiny gray kitten wandered shyly up to the bucket of suds and pitifully began to lap at the soapy water. J. shooed him away, and a chorus of protests arose: "Ooooh, the poor thing." "Look how hungry he is!" "Oh, see how he's shivering."

"Don't anyone feed him," J. warned, ". . . or he'll never leave."

Exactly! Our three daughters, as if by signal, dropped their rags, ran into the house and in half a minute brought out a feast: cream and raw eggs and bits of salami. The kitten ate ravenously, making gasping, almost sobbing sounds.

"He shouldn't eat so fast," said my youngest. "He might have to throw up." She then saw that the kitten had seven toes on one paw, and eight on the other. "Oh no, he's a misfit," she cried. "We have to adopt him, so he'll feel loved."

"Don't even consider it," J. said. "And don't give him a name."

"We'll just call him Kitty," she told him, as if to reassure him that a generic title could prevent ownership. And so she did call him Kitty. And so did her sisters. And so did I. And so he has been called ever after.

~

Now I say to him, after all these many years that he has been called, merely, "Kitty," "Don't worry, Big Kitty, we love you, too." And I realize that by naming him thus, I've just made room for one more.

December 18

At the break of dawn I am out of bed and looking around the pool deck, tying tight the belt of my pink plush bathrobe. It's freezing out here. I bend nearly upside-down to see into the crawl space, but it's dark under the house; dirt and spiders abound, it's totally inhospitable, frightening in some childhood-terror part of my mind. To think that any small, living creature is under there, shivering and starving, is almost too much for me.

"Kitty, Kitty . . ." I call softly. "Here, Little Kitty."

I hold my breath to witness nothing, the absence of sound, a negative certainty. The newspaper delivery truck comes by, its headlights washing over the pool wall, and there's the thunk of the newspaper hitting the front walk.

"Kitty?" I call again. I am almost relieved. Fine, my problem has evaporated. He's gone, run away to some other house, or found his way home. But, of course, I can't let it alone. What if he's just wandering the streets, lost and hungry? Or worse, is frozen dead under the house. How will I ever know? I imagine months passing—and in the spring, when it's warm, I will smell his decomposing body!

Now I wonder who could have turned him loose. Or possibly deposited him near or even (purposely) at my door. Has he, by some accident, escaped from a loving home and is someone at this moment grieving for a precious pet? But then—isn't it unlikely that so small an animal could dash out a door, come so far?

I suspect that someone, too kind-hearted (or too cowardly) to take a kitten, or a litter of them, to the pound where in a few days they might be gassed, would take a chance, set them down in a promising place and drive off, trusting to fate.

In this light, I assess my neighborhood; it looks pleasantly middle-class, the lawns are well-kept, the trees are old and handsome. Surely it looks as if those who live here could afford a can of cat food a day; most of us in this neighborhood do have pets.

But this is all academic. Clearly the kitten is gone, and I'm through worrying. One less problem in a life of many problems.

I go inside, stir up some frozen orange juice, start the coffee. I hear J. get up and turn on the heat. In the laundry room, I set the washing machine and hear the water start to fill. In the enamel tub are six or seven robes of my mother's that I told her yesterday (when I didn't get to give her a haircut, after all) I would launder and bring back to the nursing home today. Even though her name is written in black marker on the collar of each robe, she doesn't trust the nursing home laundry. "They steal everything they see," she says with perfect confidence. "Nothing is safe here."

~

The halls of the nursing home are decked with boughs of holly. This is her second Christmas in residence here—we know, my mother and I, what a fuss they make about Christmas. She's totally scornful: "They tell me Santa Claus is going to visit me! Do I care? Do I want to see some old guy in a red costume?"

People are flowing through the halls; this is an enormous place, this convalescent hospital. There are nine wings, comprising levels of . . . is it fair to call it . . . hell? Probably not; there are days it seems a decent place, a kind of necessary solution, if not exactly a home, for me in some ways as well as for my mother. The lower-numbered wings (100, 200, 300) are the locked wards which house the totally incompetent, the Alzheimer's patients, the violent, the aged-insane. Patients seem to be segregated by degrees of helplessness, mental and physical. In the 900 wing are just very old people (and some heartbreakingly young) who are there because they walk and fall, or have no legs at all, or because they need oxygen at all times, or because their hearts are failing or their blood vessels are too narrow to accommodate an adequate blood flow.

Many of them still socialize with one another, sit outside and talk, smoke, go to chapel, walk the halls, holding onto walkers or the handles of their wheelchairs. In the lounge there is a piano, on which, when my mother could still use her two hands, she used to play Beethoven. But my mother hasn't been in the 900 wing since August, when, by a series of accidents, she lost what she considered her human life and began, according to her, her life "as less than an animal."

Today, as I come in, the aides are punching in and out at the time clock in the hall, the aides-in-training are filing into chapel, where during the week they take classes instructing them on how to take care of the very old, the very sick, the very weak, the senile, and the dying.

I greet the receptionist at the desk, I wave to Noreen in her wheelchair—she is the MS patient who has been here for twelve years, and who has an easel and paints in her room. I pass by the beauty parlor, the little snack bar, and finally I'm at the 500 wing, the Medicare wing, where my mother is recovering . . . or not recovering. It's where she lives now, in one single bed, and occasionally sits up for an hour or two a day in a wheelchair.

She is staring at her feeding tube pump as I come in. She watches the circular arrow travel its course, round and round, twenty-four hours a day. She watches for fear it will stop spinning and she will starve to death, even though she has been assured many times that any malfunction in the equipment will set off a loud alarm. Still, she doubts the alarm will work when the time comes.

I pass by her roommate, one of many she has had, who is sleeping with her mouth open.

"Ma?" I say tentatively.

Her head moves slowly in my direction. I feel the beacon of her eyes settle on me; she takes me in, her daughter, her eldest. She opens her mouth in a soft toothless smile, not really a smile but a start of her lawyer's argument; I see her pump up her energy, up to the top of the thin tube of her body, up to her mouth, where the words gather and wait all the days between my visits or my sister's visits.

"You're just in time. I'm so glad to see you," she says, "because if I didn't have you or your sister to talk to I would lose my mind. Because otherwise I'm like an animal in a cage. Days pass and I don't have another soul in the world I can tell my troubles to."

Merrill Joan Gerber

December 19

The food bowls are empty! The ones I set out yesterday morning were still full when I came back from visiting my mother, but this morning they're licked clean!

"Kitty?" I call, but, as I expected, there's no answer. Is he exceptionally wary? Or gone? Did another creature eat the food? A possum, a raccoon? Maybe an army of termites? Still, my heart lightens, I find myself cheerfully dicing a few slices of leftover roast beef and setting the tiny pieces on a plate in the crawl hole opening.

Then I go inside to slide my feet around on the towel in front of the dishwasher. The leak is very mysterious; about three ounces of water appears at odd intervals—and not necessarily when the dishwasher is running or filling or rinsing or draining; it just happens, arbitrarily, on some private timetable of its own. J. seems to be doing a psychological study of its intentions. A plumber isn't what he thinks the leak requires; perhaps a dysfunctional-kitchen therapist. I am running out of patience, not to mention old towels. But you can't hurry a husband into action any more than you can hurry a kitten. In time, in time. All in good time.

~

My mother has always been my interpreter of reality. Her pattern over the years is to tell me first what happens, and to tell me next what it means. Yesterday she told me that an aide came in and hid behind her curtain in order to watch a soap opera on my mother's little TV, and that the meaning of this act was that "they don't want to work, why should they, they're paid nothing." When she sees life through their eyes, she's sympathetic; when they don't work in her behalf they're "lazy nothings."

Today she tells me about her shower. "They put me in a shower chair. They wheel me through the halls. I sit there naked while they talk to one another. Then they scald me. They burn me. Or they freeze me. They don't know hot from cold. They're not like us."

"What do you mean, Mom?" I say. "They're not humans?" Certain remarks I can't let her get away with.

"What do they know?" she says. "They're immigrants."

"You weren't an immigrant?"

"Certainly not," she says. "I was born in this country."

"But your parents, they were immigrants. They came here from another country, speaking another language."

"That's right, " she says. "And what did they know? Nothing!"

Today my mother lies in her bed, her white hair blending with the white of the white pillow, her pale white face faded, her old eyes watery, swimming in some deep pool of anger and memory. Her paralyzed arm is limp on the sheet; the nurse has placed a roll of gauze in her palm to keep her fingers from clenching into a claw. This woman, my mother, was once a classical pianist. "Was once" is what everyone here once was.

"So, Mom, guess what? I think a kitten is hiding under my house."

I consider this appropriate material for conversation. I always come armed with some news, after carefully editing out what might unduly disturb her, confuse her, cause anxiety, upset her. Even the leaking dishwasher is not a subject for discussion here, since she already believes nothing works as it should, and . . . if one machine can malfunction, then her feeding tube machine can also fail.

"Are you feeding it?" she asks. "You shouldn't feed it, or it will never go away."

"Why shouldn't I feed it if it's hungry?"

"Because you already have enough responsibility as it is," she says simply. "Look what I put you through. You have to come and see your sick mother all the time."

"Oh, Mom. I like to see you."

"I'd be better off dead," she states. And then the nurse comes in with a syringe of pink fluid to inject into the feeding tube.

"What am I getting now?" my mother asks.

"Medicine," the nurse says. "To make you better."

My mother rolls her eyes in my direction. When the nurse leaves, she says, "That's what they tell me: 'medicine.' Do they know how I used to keep charts of every pill I had to take, and I knew what every drug was for? If I could still write, I would keep my lists here. But that's how stupid they think I am. 'Medicine' they call it."

"Well, Mom," I say, glancing at the clock, already feeling exhausted and wondering how soon I can leave. "Medicine is as good a word as any. If it helps you, it's medicine."

"Nothing helps me," she says to me. "I'll be here the rest of my life, won't I?"

I look around at the feeding tube, at the catheter delivering her urine into a bag, at her paralyzed arm, at her useless legs.

"Maybe," I say. "I don't really know." The pang of guilt that always hovers above me hits down and I feel a headache start to throb in my temple. *Could she live with me? Should she?*

She sees me look at the clock again. "What do you have to do when you leave here?"

"Shop," I say. "We're completely out of food. There's nothing to eat at home." I say it as if there isn't a single potato in the house, not a piece of bread, not a dry sliver of meat. I say it as if we're all about to starve to death in my house; if I don't fill the larder there will be gruesome results, skeletons will be discovered on the floor after the police break down the door.

"Then go," she says. "Or you'll be too tired to shop."

"Yes, I'll go," I say, gratefully. I lean over and kiss her pale forehead. It feels damp and cool . . . not healthy. She doesn't kiss me back; she has never been a kisser.

"Don't carry heavy things," she says. "You don't want to hurt yourself."

"No, I won't. Don't worry, Mom." No one else cares about me this way. No one else loves me the way she does. I back away toward the door, waving, throwing a last kiss, and then—as the teenagers say—I'm out of there! I walk down the hall, I walk fast, I nearly run till I reach the door, which I fling outward and draw breath in the sunshine. Escaped again. Free at last.

December 21

I have found the food bowls empty for three days in a row; empty twice a day, in fact, since I now put out food toward evening as well. Yet when I call, cajole, trill, beg, wheedle and summon the Underground Mystery Kitten, I see and hear nothing. Well, I have patience. I have food. Maybe I will win out.

J. knows nothing of this battle of wills going on. He sees me going out to the pool deck often; I always carry a dripping towel from under the dishwasher and eventually bring back a stiff and dry one from the pool wall. He must be aware that one day I will override his wishes and call the plumber, but we don't discuss it. We've had a long marriage and I know our patterns. In the end I always do call a plumber—or an electrician, or a carpenter, depending on the problem. But a period of time must always pass during which J. knows I know he is thinking about how he might fix the problem, and I am letting him see that I am letting him think.

However, finally a moment of crisis arrives at which point he knows my tolerance for the philosophical approach to home repairs has run out and a showdown is inevitable. I can tell we have reached a truce when he indicates by some casual gesture that yes, maybe I better call the guy who knows what to do.

In every marriage there must be these power struggles; at least in ours, we have worked out a pattern that involves the least violence.

Once I have the go-ahead signal, I call the repairman, make the date, fortify myself against being overcharged. But in this way, J. and I avoid confrontations, and a kind of harmony ensues from following our long-tested pattern.

If, indeed, we do have a new kitten in our lives, it is my hope that J. will let the issue rest, not insist on our freedom from new and additional responsibilities. We'll have to see.

It may be that this is only a phantom cat, anyway, the equivalent of a false pregnancy. I may have imagined the whole thing, out of pure need.

I begin to stand watch outside. Or sit watch. I sit on one of the hardbacked wrought-iron chairs that go with the little glass table near the pool. I watch the bowls I have set on the dirt inside the crawl space. I wonder if perhaps armies of ants carry off the food and that nothing larger than a cockroach lives under the house. I worry that the kitten is stuck among pipes or caught under a concrete piling, or has frozen and turned into a marble statue. At one point I go into the house and call the fire department of our city, and ask if they would come out to rescue a kitten from under the house. The fireman says kindly, "We don't do that kind of thing anymore, ma'am. We have budget problems. But I'll tell you, if a kitten gets hungry enough, it will come out from anywhere, from an attic, from a tree, from down in a sewer. So don't you worry. If you don't see it, it's probably long gone."

Today as I sit outside in the cold, watching the pool water ripple and skim as the pump pulls the water into the filter (we never swim in the winter; the cost of gas for heating the pool is too high), I decide I will put the bowl of food on the back door step instead of in the crawl space. Perhaps I will be able to seduce him out into the world.

I set down a bowl of chicken scraps on the step just beneath the pool door. Then I stand inside, looking out through the small glass window in the door, and I wait. I wait. I wait. I begin to understand the virtue of stillness, of patience. I think of those who meditate on mountain tops, breathe in, breathe out, wait for enlightenment.

I begin to count leaves floating on the surface of the pool, to count the threads of a spider web in the mock orange tree, to count the shopping days to Christmas. My daughter, Joanna, will be flying home tomorrow from graduate school in the East. Oh, how delightful it would be if we had a new kitten here to welcome her!

And suddenly I see a flash of fur in the corner of my eye. There it is! It's come out, drawn by the aroma of barbecued chicken! It pulls a morsel of meat off the plate and hops back with it under the house. (By squashing my face against the glass, I can just see the edge of the hole under the house.)

In my mind I replay what I have just seen. The wildcat speed of his appearance and disappearance. And something else. A flash of a high-held rump, a tiny stump but not a tail. Almost a rabbit's gait as he runs away. But no tail! Deformed! My kitten has been maimed or injured. Someone has chopped off his tail! Oh the poor baby. My heart goes out to him. *Little Kitty*, I think, *What you need is love. What you need is a hug from me.*

December 22

Today Joanna arrives! Late tonight we will meet her at the Hilton Hotel, where the airport bus drops her off. All our family's parting scenes and homecoming reunions take place on the sidewalk in front of this hotel; I am sure the doormen cast an indifferent eye upon all the comings and goings, but for me just the sight of that hotel makes me pull out a handkerchief.

I will be so happy to see Joanna, our middle daughter, who has not been home since the end of summer, and who has not really lived at home since going off to college so many years ago. I remember a vision of that day—was she seventeen or eighteen then?—wearing red cotton shorts, her hair in a long braid, kissing me goodbye and climbing into a car with another girl from her high school also going away to Stanford. The girl's mother, who was delivering them in person, assured me she'd see that they were safely settled. On the roof of the car was an upside-down bicycle; visible through the windows were the requisite guitars, pillows, tennis rackets, stereo players, books, stuffed animals. I waved them off, smiling bravely, then swam home through a waterfall of tears, and sat in my child's empty room for an hour, sobbing, while at the same time noticing a few unpaired socks tossed among the dustballs in the bottom of her closet, then picking up a few ratty tissues from under her desk, finally getting busy and changing the sheets on her bed in anticipation of her visit home at Christmas.

I've toughened up since then; Joanna's room is where we keep the computer now. In fact, since all three of our girls are gone, the oldest married and the other two in graduate school, I've come to appreciate my empty house, the privacy I now share with J., my being excused from the daily worries of being a mother, not to mention the relief from laundry and cooking for five. (The worries never go away, of course, but are now of the general cosmic sort, since I don't know what the children are doing from day to day.)

My first act of the morning is to check the bowls of food on the step. Once again they're empty. Our Invisible Visitor is getting bolder. I decide it's time to put into effect my new plan: I fry up some chicken livers, cut in small pieces, and set them—still steaming and fragrant—out on the step at the pool deck.

I hope it doesn't take too long, since I have a great deal to do today. I set myself in viewing position at some distance from the crawl space and from the step, but I do sit unhidden, without disguise, fully visible. However, I don't have to wait too long. As daunting as I may appear as I sit there reading a magazine, feigning indifference to whatever may occur, the chicken livers must attract in greater magnetic force than I repel. The kitten, with a little cry of doubt, finally ventures forth into the light of day and grabs a morsel of liver. Before he darts underground, I see him quite clearly: he's tiny, but oh! he's magnificent! His coat is smoky-gray, shimmering with black stripes. I am left with the impression of great round green eyes, a delicate triangular face. And speed! He is liquid lightning.

I laugh out loud. He's so little, so cute, so clever, so fast! Racing away to carry to some private place his prize, the chicken liver! At this moment he is devouring what a cat must desire most—the soft, delicious entrails of *Bird*, his lifelong enemy. Even in a life so short as his, this kitten has enemies he hasn't even made yet.

I go inside to do some of my chores, feeling victorious.

~

J. and I are having dinner, discussing when to leave for the Hilton, when I jump up to call the airline to make sure the plane is on time. To my dismay, I hear that "there has been a medical emergency

Merrill Joan Gerber

onboard, and the plane had to make an emergency landing in Kansas City." I am told to call later to find out when the plane will get into Los Angeles.

I tell J. what has happened. "What are the odds," I ask him, "that the medical emergency could be Joanna?"

"Zero," he says. "Not a chance."

So—it's clear I can't worry in his presence. Fathers are simply not well-trained in worrying. I have suddenly lost my appetite, so I take my chicken wing and carry it outside.

"Here, Tilly," I say, waving it around in the crawl space hole, tilting it this way and that to disseminate its aroma. "Come and get it." Why I call him "Tilly" I cannot say. It comes easily to the tongue. It sounds close, somehow, to "Kitty." I realize if this cat becomes mine, I will have to give him a real name. "Come and get your chicken!" I lay the wing on the step outside the pool door and stand there.

How fast his head pops up! Oh, I see what has happened: he is hooked on the flavor of chicken! He peers up at me from the crawl space hole. Clearly, he's torn about what to do next. He steps forward and then runs away; comes back, tentatively looks at me, then runs away to hide. But he's urgently hungry, too. He doesn't know what to do. He runs forward and spins around. He runs and spins. His head and tail—or the place where his tail would be—seem to trade places. I can't help laughing out loud.

"Oh, come here and have some chicken," I say, bending down and laying on the cement a few filaments of chicken flesh.

And the kitten is overcome by desire. He loses all sense of caution and plunges forward to seize the chicken, and as he does so, I seize him!

How light he is, how small. And how frightened! He sizzles with fear, struggling in my hands, straining to flee, to hide, to be safe under the dark, cold house.

But I will not let go of this prize. I carry him triumphantly into the house, and into the line of vision of J., who is finishing his chicken dinner.

My husband stares in puzzlement, as if he is trying to understand how Big Kitty could have shrunk to such a miniature arrangement of limbs and body.

"Oh," I say ingenuously. "This little kitten seems to be lost." I realize the time is ripe, I can no longer keep this a secret. I must initiate the delicate program to win J. over: "I found him starving out by the pool. Look how he's shivering with cold. I have to feed him something or he'll die."

"You're not going to keep him!" (It's not exactly a question.)

"Of course not. But I have to figure out what to do . . . tomorrow." I change the subject. "I'll call the airport and see what the situation is now."

Clutching the kitten in my iron grip, I use the kitchen phone. Luckily, the medical emergency in Kansas City is over, the plane is on its way again. However, it will be coming in too late for Joanna to catch the airport bus to the Hilton, so we'll have to drive all the way to the airport to meet her at midnight.

"Let's get ready," I tell J. While he is getting on his shoes, I carry the kitten into the garage and locate a carton and a soft pillow for his bed.

"Oh, kitten, kitten, my kitten." Am I this dottily happy about my child coming home, or my kitten coming in?

I kiss the kitten on his striped forehead, noting the beautiful raccoon mask drawn on the sides of his face, noting again the strange, cropped look of his tail-less rump. His fur is silken, shimmering. My heart calms as I stroke him. He's afraid, but he's watching me with interest, too. I put the box with him in it in the laundry room with some bits of chicken and a bowl of water. I am imagining what Joanna will say when I reveal him to her. She will scream with delight! She will hug me.

Just to think of the surprise to come makes me jump for joy like a five-year-old! When, I wonder, did I last feel this much hope and happiness?

December 23

Of course she's the last one off the plane. But there she is, smiling a sweet wide grin, her heavy book bag over her shoulder, her clothes disheveled, her long hair in wild curls that nearly obliterate our view of her face. She has to toss a lock of it back, and back again, to see us.

I can't quite get over the fact that she's here via the miracle of flight. Just a few hours ago she was in New Haven; now she's in Los Angeles. I never take it for granted; each time I see the round black nose of a plane pulling up to the docking platform, I gasp with gratitude that it has safely delivered my daughter.

All those miles it has to fly, unsupported, not plugged in to any power source, with only air beneath and above it—it's probably an aberration of physics, and one day will be proved impossible.

We smile, we kiss and hug. I kiss and hug first, long and hard, her father is second in line. For some reason, whenever J. kisses our children, he always pats them on the back, in the way one might console a child.

We ask her about the medical emergency. Our daughter tells us a man fell ill, fainted, needed oxygen; the attendants feared heart attack, and radioed for permission to land at the nearest airport. After the man was carried off, a long delay ensued while a new oxygen tank was ordered for the plane, which is forbidden by law to fly without one.

But now she is here, exhausted, happy. (By the hour in her time zone, it is well after 3:00 a.m.) After we collect her luggage from the carousel and load it in the car, she collapses in the back seat, and I, in the front seat, hold her hand by reaching backwards over my head. I am totally happy, to be holding my child's hand in mine. All other considerations recede in the clear rightness of this union. We belong together. She is mine.

~

At home, she marvels at how different the house looks. (We have a new light fixture over the kitchen table; maybe a few new knick-knacks, a different chair in the living room. But she has been gone a long time.) I offer snacks, chocolate pudding pie, baked apples, noodle pudding, things I have been preparing all day.

There is no sound from the laundry room; I am reserving the moment to unveil the kitten, but his silence worries me. Is he alive? Could he have managed somehow to open the clothes washer and turn it on, fill it up, dive in, and drown? Or, failing that, could he have got into the dryer, heated himself up to a hollow fluff of fur? I have heard horror stories: of kittens who fall asleep in clothes dry-ers and meet their fate in a load of diapers, or kittens who hide in microwave ovens and explode into smithereens.

I don't want to rush in and find him expired; after all, my daugh-ter has already been through one medical emergency tonight. On the other hand, I can hardly contain myself, imagining her delighted reaction when I throw open the door and present the new arrival. (On the other *other* hand, however, J. may have forgotten the kitten by now, and will be surprised and annoyed all over again!)

I bide my time, wait till my daughter has eaten some food, told us about the schoolwork she has to do over the break, wait till J. yawns and says he is going in to get ready for bed (and walks out of the kitchen), and finally I say, "Come over here with me, I want to show you something."

Joanna comes willingly, a little tentatively, possibly thinking that the only thing in the laundry room could be a new piece of laundry equipment. I hum a little fanfare and slide open the door.

And there he is, on the floor in his box, curled adorably, his green eyes blinking in worry and apprehension.

"Oh Mom!" she cries. "Oh, how beautiful! Oh, how sweet and wonderful. Whose is he? Oh, can I pick him up?" She bends slowly, crooning, and scoops up the kitten in her arms, she cradles him to her breast, she whispers in his ear.

I am faint with happiness. There is no moment quite like this in my memory; it's been so long since I have delighted a child of mine.

"Oh Mom," my daughter says again. "Can we keep him?"

~

In the morning Joanna and I sit over French toast and coffee, making lists of cat names. J. has gone off to teach his classes at the college.

"What about Harvey?" Joanna says.

"I sort of like Tilly," I suggest. "It sounds a little like Kitty."

"But what if he's not a she?"

"Does it really matter?"

"We should try to figure it out. I think it makes a difference."

The animal in question has disappeared into the recesses of the house. He's too little to find, too ingenious; we will just have to wait till he emerges.

Joanna says, "Let's proceed as if he's a he," she says. "What about Huey, or Louie, or Dewey?"

"What about Ivan, Igor, or Boris?"

"Mischa? Alyosha?"

We burst out laughing. We each make a list and compare them. On mine is Velvel (which is my father's Yiddish name), Sebastian, Arturo, Georgio. On Joanna's is Axel, Zack, Hazel (in case he is a she), Calvin, Hobbes, and Andy. We try out Tiger, Lightning, Twitchy, Salty, and like none of them.

At noon, our daughter Susanna calls from Berkeley and we tell her about the new family member. For a name she suggests "Geordie." It feels right to her, she says. We determine the name *has* to have an "ee" sound at the end, for ease in . . . what? In sounding like our first cat's name, Korky, perhaps.

Joanna and I hunt through the house for the kitten; just when we are ready to give up, she cries out, "There he is," and he climbs out, looking wary, from the open pot cabinet under the stove.

"Come here, Ivan," I say, approaching slowly, but in a split second he has run to hide under the couch. Joanna and I follow him, get flat on our bellies to see his gleaming eyes staring back at us.

"Here, Hazel," she calls.

"Here, Mortimer," I ask of him. "Or Tilly."

"We could call him Generic," Joanna says. "Genny for short."

"Notail is a possibility."

"No, it isn't," she says. "Think of it, Mom. Could you see yourself calling, 'Notail, Notail'?"

"I'm getting dizzy thinking already," I say. "Would you like to visit Mom-Mom at the nursing home?"

"Sure," Joanna says. "Let me take a shower and I'll be ready in fifteen minutes. Maybe by then he'll have come out."

~

He does finally come out, by virtue of a saucer of cream held to the underside of the couch, and once he's in our grasp, Joanna and I decide to take the kitten to see my mother. We recognize the value of having an agenda, some way to focus the visit to distract her from her catalog of complaints.

Joanna hasn't seen my mother since last summer, when—in the period of one week—she suffered both a stroke and a broken hip. Joanna was at my side when the orthopedic surgeon said to us, "This woman's life is hanging by a thread. Once an old person breaks a hip, she knows in her bones, no pun intended, that she's destined to fall again and probably break the other hip."

As we drive to the nursing home, I am thinking about the day my mother threw the plate of liver at the wall. My mother was already living there when the incident occurred, though she had not yet had the stroke or broken her hip. (By comparison to her present life, her existence then was relatively acceptable. She could walk, and take herself to the bathroom, feed herself, use her hands perfectly well and play the piano in the activity room. She often sat outside with other residents to take the sun.) What had brought her there were various complications of poor circulation: a gangrenous toe at first, then the need to recover from femoral artery bypass surgery which increased the blood flow to her foot, and saved it from being amputated.

On the day Joanna and I visited, she had no warning that we were coming. We walked in, expecting that she'd be glad to see us, but she was staring at her food tray, her face dark with fury, her mouth and eyes three fierce holes. When we greeted her, she looked up and began to yell: "This is food a dog wouldn't eat! You call this liver? This is poison! Look at this garbage!" She stabbed at the meal with a fork, then threw the plate across the room so that food splattered everywhere. "Burned black! A rock! Even the aide couldn't cut it for me, no knife would go through it. They do it to save money, they serve garbage here." Then, realizing that her granddaughter was witnessing this melodrama, she said, "I'm sorry you have to see me this way, Joanna."

Now I look over toward Joanna as we drive to the nursing home. "Lucky that my mother doesn't have to eat liver anymore," I say.

"I hope she'll be calm today," Joanna says. "The day she threw the liver—it was like she was possessed. She had no control over her own behavior."

"The scary thing about getting old is that you see yourself losing control over *everything*," I tell her. "It's not a pretty thought."

"Maybe she'll be in a good mood today. Today we have the kitten with us!"

Joanna taps gently on the cardboard carry-case (left over from Big Kitty's and Korky's trips to the vet). Our kitten is silent, huddled down in a small ball of fur, trying to become invisible. It seems to be a survival technique, to be so still that the predators will pass by without discovering him.

⁓

"We brought you a visitor, Mom-Mom," I say. My mother's eyes are closed. Her face, her hair, are white on the pillow. Slowly she opens her eyes, they focus, a light dawns in them. But she doesn't smile.

"It's Joanna," I say, not sure she has recognized that I've brought Joanna with me.

"Joanna," she says. "Look what's become of your grandmother."

"I'm sorry, Mom-Mom," she says, and moves closer as if to kiss her.

"Don't kiss me," my mother says. "You don't want to catch *this*." She looks up at me. "What exactly is wrong with me?" she asks, the same question she asks every time I visit her.

"You had a stroke, Mom. You broke your hip. And you stopped eating, so they gave you this feeding tube."

"I don't remember any of that. Why did I have a stroke?"

I brace myself against my own impatience and repeat the litany I recount almost every time I visit. She can't seem to remember it, but she's entitled to know the sequence of her downfall.

"Last August, Mom, you complained of terrible pains across your stomach. You were already living here. The doctor couldn't figure out what was causing the pain, so he had you admitted to the hospital. They gave you many complicated tests, and they were all negative. Then, one morning, the red blisters of shingles appeared on your stomach, and they understood that that was the source of your pain. But by then they had given you so much medication—tranquilizers and pills to lower your blood pressure—that it may have caused the stroke, which paralyzed your right hand."

"What is shingles? I forgot."

"It's some kind of virus, like the chicken pox virus. It lives in your nerve endings and when your resistance is low, it seems to break out and attack you. And it's very painful."

"And what's a stroke?" my mother asks.

I sigh. Joanna and I look at one another.

The woman in the next bed snorts. She says, "Your mother asks the nurse these questions every day. I have a stroke, but my mind is fine."

"Oh, tell her to shut up," my mother says to me.

Joanna looks disturbed. She doesn't realize how little courtesy is left in any of the old people by this point in their lives. (I must admit, though, that my mother has *never* been particularly mindful of the feelings of others.)

"A stroke means that the blood supply to the brain is cut off, and some brain cells die. In your case, Ma, it affected your right hand."

"It should have killed me," my mother says reasonably. "This is no way to live. Why can't I walk? The stroke didn't go to my legs, did it?"

"No, it didn't. But you were heavily sedated, and you didn't know where you were, the nurses hadn't restrained you to the bed, so one morning you had to go to the bathroom, and you got up, and you fell."

"You should sue them!" my mother's roommate calls out. "You should sue every one of the bastards."

"We thought of it," I tell her, "but we didn't have the energy."

"Sue them all," my mother's roommate mutters.

"I'll sue *you* if you don't stop interrupting us," my mother says.

"Mom," I interject. "Aren't you going to ask Joanna how she is? She's just come all the way home from Yale."

"How are you, darling?" my mother says. "I'm happy to see you, but don't kiss me."

"I won't. But we brought you a surprise."

"I hope it isn't food. You know I don't eat anything by mouth. I get all my food through this tube."

"It isn't food."

"It's in this box," I add, lifting up the carry-case and setting it at the foot of my mother's bed. We hear a scuffling inside.

"I hope it's not a snake!" my mother cries.

"No, no, it's just a sweet baby kitten." I open the box and pull out our treasure. I want to put the kitten on my mother's breast, the way they offer newborn infants to a mother who has just given birth.

"Oh, take it away," she says, truly frightened. "If it scratches me, I can't protect myself."

"He's very gentle," I plead. "Touch him with your good hand, Ma."

"I can't even wash my hands," she says. "Don't force me! Please!" She seems close to tears.

I withdraw the kitten from her and bring his little face toward my own. "Ma, he's as scared of you as you are of him. He was lost. We found him starving under the house. He was so lonely, and afraid.

He was helpless and had nowhere to go. He was so miserable."

"Like me," my mother says. "Trapped and helpless."

I feel like crying in frustration because she can't see anything but her own plight. I put my face against the kitten's silken fur, I kiss the tip of his heart-shaped pink nose. If she refuses to take comfort in him, I will. I have to.

"What are you naming him?"

"I don't know."

"Then why don't you call him Maximilian?" she says. "Maxie, My Million. Remember how Daddy used to call you *his* million? Well, this kitten can be your million."

"I guess it's the only way I'll ever have a million." I try to smile. And then we all laugh. My mother, her roommate, Joanna, and I— we laugh. We keep laughing because it's so much better a feeling than nearly crying.

"So that's his name," my mother says. "You'll call him Maxie. Maximilian for formal events. Maxie for all other occasions."

Merrill Joan Gerber

December 24

With pets come responsibilities. Now that we have staked claim to Maxie and brought him inside, he must have proper quarters. He must have a litter box, he must have litter. He must have a collar and even—now that he has a name—a name tag. He must have cat food, or kitten food at least, and he must have bowls of his own out of which to eat.

Therefore, Joanna and I need to go shopping! It's a fitting time of year to have this impulse—this frenzy before Christmas—and today there is the added mania of frenzy that takes place the last few hours before Christmas Eve. We don't have Christmas at our house, both to our relief and occasional disappointment. We celebrated Chanukah when the children were small, but now J. and I write them each a check; they know what they want and we don't.

Today we shut Maxie in the laundry room and set out to shop. I tell Joanna that we'll probably find no Christmas shoppers at the pet store, but how wrong I am! The cash register is jingling madly; people are buying dog toys and cat toys, dog houses and cat condominiums. There are four-foot-long rubber bones, flavored with an aromatic meaty smell! There are golden balls with little yellow toy birds caged inside them. There are dog books and cat books, dog and cat greeting cards, even dog and cat (not to mention parrot and fish) jewelry. This is not only a store for pet supplies, it is a store that supplies gifts for people who love pets.

Joanna and I examine the array of litter boxes, which now come enclosed in cabinets (for those with delicate sensibilities) in all colors of the rainbow, large and small, hinged and not hinged. Litter itself offers staggering variety. It comes as chipped stone, sand, or clay, with and without deodorant, of the clumping and non-clumping variety. It comes in slate gray or dotted with green particles, it is sold with litter liners or without.

We browse through the aisles of food—formulated for young, medium, and old animals—of collars and leashes, of sweaters and rainwear, of vitamins and yeast supplements, of bath products, flea sprays, tools for grooming, for nail clipping, for brushing and combing. We examine ID tags shaped as bones, shaped as individual breeds of dogs and cats, shaped as happy faces. There are even computer chips that can be implanted—but only by a veterinarian—in an animal's skin. My daughter and I look at one another and burst out laughing. Unable to decide on a single item, we leave the store. One day we may want to buy Maxie one of those four-story abodes, with scratching post on the bottom, and stair-step layers going up to the ceiling, one for napping in the round, one in the square, one on a flat pedestal surface. One day, maybe . . . only not yet. Mainly we want to get home as fast as we can to see and embrace our little kitten.

～

Maxie is sleeping snugly in the carton in the laundry room. *"Oh, how cute, how cute!"* we say. What is "cute"? It is all that he is, very small, very soft, very beautiful, very much ours. We admire out loud the designs of his fur, the artful swirls and stripes, the kaleidoscopic patterns; the heart-shaped pink pad of his nose, the tiny upturned curl of his lips (his smile!), the soft black cushions of his paws. He seems to have been designed to be adored.

My daughter and I admire him as if he were made out of sunshine, out of flowers and trees, out of stars. We can't believe he was dispensable to someone who had no space for him, no heart for him, no home for him.

We hear J. approaching and exchange a meaningful glance. Joanna waits till he is in his chair at the kitchen table, eating some peanuts. Then she scoops Maxie up in her arms and deposits him in J.'s lap.

"Isn't he cute, Daddy?" J. looks as if we have just dumped a tub of raw fish in his lap. My heart goes out to him; a man who never had a pet in childhood is truly disadvantaged. We are going to try to remedy this now, with utmost tact and delicacy.

"Look how he loves you," I say, stretching it a bit. But it's almost true: Maxie looks up at him with trust, with interest. J. gingerly pats the top of his head, keeping his fingers as far away from claws and teeth as he can get. Maxie tilts his head; his pink tongue shoots out and licks J.'s fingers. Well, that's enough for one session. I lift Maxie off J.'s lap.

"You're not really thinking of keeping him, are you? I mean, we have a cat, don't we? Isn't one enough?"

"Maybe he has an owner," I tell him. "If the owner advertises in the paper, we'll see the ad. But if this kitten was abandoned, we can't take him to the pound where they'll put him to sleep, can we? So we may have to adopt him. But don't worry—he can live outside with Kitty. He won't be any trouble. He won't cost much to keep. It's just that we can't let him live outside yet. He's too little. And it's too cold out. But he can stay in the laundry room—don't worry."

J. seems mollified. He nods and goes back to eating peanuts. Joanna and I grin at each other. Then we make dinner together; roast chicken and sweet potatoes, with a special foil pan in which to bake the giblets for Maxie.

December 31

Company has arrived for the New Year's weekend: J.'s sister and brother-in-law, as well as their five-year-old granddaughter, Sasha, who must seem to Maxie like The Visitor From Hell. The refrain of her song is "Can I hold the kitty?" and Maxie's reply is to dash wildly for cover as soon as she comes his way with her arms held out. Much of the action involves Sasha's wiggling under or behind furniture to drag Maxie out by the paw or by the head, accompanied by lectures from the adults on humane treatment of animals. We all remind her that he lived under the house as "a wild animal" and is still frightened of people, with admonitions (since she tends to hold him around the neck with an iron grip) to pet him gently and then put him back in his box in the laundry room.

Joanna has made Maxie some toys fashioned after the models we saw in the pet supply store: a shoulder pad rolled up and tied onto a string (she titles this "The Killer Shoulder Pad"), a plastic film canister with two pennies inside it, and an old Ping-Pong ball she rolls across the floor for him to chase.

Joanna seems to be the only one able to coax Maxie out from his hiding place; once she has his attention, she keeps it by running in a circle, dragging the shoulder pad around and around on the floor. He crouches, he pounces, he spins in circles, he leaps, he attacks. We try to take him seriously, although the passion with which he undertakes these hunting expeditions causes us to burst out laughing.

I see Big Kitty looking in the sliding glass door; his nose is pressed against the glass like a child's at a candy store window. But no—when I invite him in, he backs away and turns to run into the yard. There are too many people in the house, too many strangers. And one is a little girl with glittering eyes, also ready to pounce.

∾

In the afternoon, we put Maxie in the laundry room, kiss him good-bye, and all of us leave the house to visit the site of the Rose Float. In our nearby park, where they build the float each year, citizens of our city gather to deck it with flowers, glue on leaves, seeds, bark, husks, and any manner of plant material. Just before midnight, in a fanfare of applause and shouts of "Good Luck" the float will roll out into the street and be taken to its place in the lineup for the great Rose Parade that starts at 8:00 a.m. on New Year's morning.

Sasha is jumping with excitement. The float, as usual, features cartoon-like animals, all looking friendly, antic, with wagging tails, flapping wings, clacking bills—this is a good-natured float from a small town. Tomorrow morning, on television, we will see the truly heroic floats, made by major corporations, invented with the finest technology, artistry, and beauty that real money can buy, and far beyond anything our city's modest float can boast. In the past the corporate floats have featured showboats whose turning wheels spin water, ice skaters turning and jumping on real ice, dragons breathing fire, acrobats on high wires.

Year after year, J. and I promise ourselves we will really go in *person* to the parade; stake out our places the night before, camp on the street, light the coals in the hibachi, cook hot dogs in the open air, sleep in sleeping bags, rain or shine. (Though legend has it that it never rains on the day of the Rose Parade.) But we never do go in person. We convince one another it's too cold and windy out there, it's a long night on hard cement, revelers tend to drink too much, gunshots have been known to punctuate the night (and occasionally a person).

We know: folks come from across America to see this parade, even from Europe! And we, who live less than five miles away, prefer to watch it on New Year's morning from the comfort of our big bed. Well, we are not so young as the youngsters.

We have, at least, walked down to the park to see the float being built for the last twenty-five years. Our daughters were so small when we first began the tradition; smaller, even, than Sasha is now. I think on the sameness of the years, and yet how their passing changes everything.

Sasha begs to be allowed to run under the float to pick up a fallen rose. Her grandmother says she may not, it's too dangerous to be there among the tools and hammers and glue. But she's determined . . . she wants, she wants . . . she must have! Now she is throwing a small tantrum, demanding, begging, twisting out of her grand-father's grip, beginning to cry in frustration.

"What do you want?" we all ask her in one voice.

"I want to go back to the house. I want to hold the kitten. I love him. He's better than any dumb parade float!"

January 1

It is the New Year. This morning the house is filled with noise, laughter, conversation, the ringing of the phone, and above it all the squeals of Sasha. How urgently she cries out as she chases Maxie from one end of the house to another. Her grandparents urge her to come and sit with them on the couch; the Rose Parade is on! If she watches closely, she will see the float that we saw being built last night at the park. The child runs in and assesses the attraction of what's on TV. She hesitates. She knows that sitting down is the price she will have to pay if she wants to watch.

I take this opportunity to suggest to Joanna that perhaps it's time for us to let Maxie make his acquaintance with the back yard; his knowledge of the outside, as far as we know, extends only to his hiding place under the house.

Privately, out of earshot of our guests, we debate the safety of this proposition, conjecturing that if we were Maxie, and Sasha were stalking us, and we were let outside, we'd make a break for freedom and never come back!

Even so, we decide to chance it. Although Maxie has been immaculate and correct in using his litter box, we hope that eventually he will become an inside/outside cat; if that's our goal, a gradual introduction to the outdoors is in order.

Joanna carries Maxie gently outside to the patio. (Sasha, who has been seduced by the visions on the screen, is now dubiously watching the New Year's Day parade on television, thus giving us all a brief respite from her enthusiasm.)

"Should we try to create some kind of leash for him?" Joanna asks me. "So he doesn't run away?"

"No, let's just set him down. I don't think he'll go far."

At first he's very shy, very slow to explore. He sniffs around the plastic legs of the picnic table, stays close to our feet, sees a beetle and paws at it. He gives off an amazing aura of having been born yesterday, of newness; he emits the rare quality of being a "blank slate," save for his instincts and the slight amount of worldly experience he had before we found him (the nature of which we will never know).

But something suddenly startles him; a car motor starting up, or the sliding scrape of the glass door which J. is opening to invite us in to see our city's float, coming up next in the parade.

In any case, Maxie tenses, and, without a hesitation, he darts away. In a fraction of a second, he is gone from our sight!

"Where is he?" Joanna gasps. "Where did he go?"

"I think he went that way!"

"No, I think he went the other way."

But we truly have no idea. We've lost him, that fast! That easily! We both stare around in dismay. Already I am telling myself, Well, he would surely have been a lot of trouble. J. doesn't really want another cat. I won't have to worry about fleas. I won't . . . .

But even as I am thinking these thoughts, I am dashing around the yard, peering under bushes, unable to believe that it might be over, this long life of love I have been projecting, anticipating, this community between myself and a creature of nature, this friendship with a spirit so sweet, so curious, so lively, so dear, as Maxie.

Joanna looks crestfallen; she may blame herself. I know I am blaming *my*self. He was too immature to take outside, he didn't know yet where his home was and now he'll never find it again. We call and we wheedle and we snap our fingers and we talk baby talk, but all is silence. No Maxie. Gone into the wilds. To be torn to bits by vultures, by predators. Soon to be starving and freezing in the bitter night. Wondering why we, who knew better, let him go. We are guilty of Cat Abuse! Of cruelty, abandonment, indifference.

Oh, I can't believe the shape of the future can be changed like this, in the blink of an eye. I realize I had been counting on his presence, his warmth, his delight in life. Now I see only a long winter ahead, of bleak visits to the nursing home, of visions of the end of life, the long, sorry, decline, the approach of death. (My mother's. Mine.) I see myself alone; the guests gone home, Joanna gone back to graduate school, J. gone off to teach his classes, and myself at the window, staring out at the rain (there *can* be rain in California), imagining Maxie, skeleton-thin, poking through the scraps near a garbage can somewhere, wondering what happened to his killer-shoulder pad, his Ping-Pong ball, his soft pillow.

Sasha shocks me out of my reverie. "I want to hold the kitty!" she cries.

"He's missing," Joanna tells her. "He ran away. Even we can't find him."

"He's not here anymore?" she says, her eyebrows coming up in a most forlorn expression. "Then my whole visit is ruined," she concludes. "My whole New Year is ruined."

∼

All during the long day, during the rest of the parade, during the Rose Bowl game, during a dull dinner of tuna fish casserole, we take turns scouring the back yard, calling Maxie's name.

"Maxie!"

"Here, Maxie, pussy, pussy, baby."

"C'mere big Max."

"Food time, Maxie."

"Come to Sasha, Maxie, I'll tell you a story. I'll tickle you."

Nothing. It is growing dark now. It's getting cold. It's no use. He's ten blocks away by now. He's been hit by a car. He's been eaten by an owl. Two dogs have taken him prisoner. I am losing it. I excuse myself and decide to take to my bed for a half hour, exhausted. J.'s sister asks if she and Sasha may make Jell-O, as an activity to entertain Sasha. I agree happily, getting out the box and the pot. Sasha complains: "I like to make it, but I hate to eat it. Jell-O is too flexible to be a good dessert!"

I wave and disappear, leaving them to deal with this flexible food. I wish that I myself were more flexible. I understand that having company is not a passive task, like having a cold and waiting for it to be over. In order to enjoy it, one must be of peaceful temperament and in a balanced state of mind. (And indeed, when is that situation ever present, in anyone's life?) Having company means putting on hold one's own projects for a time, putting aside one's ongoing arguments with one's mate, and one's petulant or childish modes. There is a need to be cheerful, attentive, good-humored, efficient. There needs to be enough clean towels in the bathroom, enough food in the refrigerator, enough chairs at the dinner table.

In return, I think, one's guests should always make it known exactly how long they are staying as well as the hour, if not the minute, of their planned departure.

J.'s sister and her husband, however, are relaxed, easygoing guests; they are agreeable, patient, they take their own coffee and toast in the mornings, are as willing to eat out as to have me make a four-course dinner; in fact, they're more than willing to treat us to lunch or dinner (or both) at a nearby restaurant. J.'s sister has even volunteered to cook dinner at my house.

Still, for me, having guests requires a form of mental control that I do not always have. I especially do not have it this minute, when my precious kitten has disappeared. And, in fact, whose disappearance may be directly related to our having house guests.

In fact, at my door this minute, comes the knocking, knocking of a small fist.

"Can I come in? It's Sasha!"

"What do you want? I'm resting."

"I need sardines," she says. "I promise you I'll find the kitten if you give me sardines. Jell-O won't work."

I can't help but laugh. "Okay, sweetheart," I say, throwing back the covers and getting up. "I'll be right there. How can I refuse if you promise you'll find him?"

~

So we fan out into the yard, all of us, J., his sister, her husband,

Joanna, Sasha, and I, all of us in a line not two feet apart, each one holding a little paper plate on which is one small, dead, silvery sardine. We are a determined search party. The men carry flashlights, though there is some faint moonlight. I imagine, for some reason, that we are all actually carrying flickering candles, and that this is a funeral procession. In a moment I will be asked to say a eulogy for our dead kitten. But he was so young! What would I say of him? That he was sweet, tender, vulnerable, spirited, brave, fuzzy, adorable, fierce? That he was my new hope, that he (unlike my mother, who was about endings) was about beginnings. That finding him had opened my heart again to hope, laughter, love? I flick away these thoughts, counting them sentimental and excessive. I feel a bug on my arm.

"Oh, he's here!" Sasha cries. "He's right here!"

And we all stop in our tracks. We listen. Sure enough, we hear a faint, pathetic "meow." We wait, and it comes again from deep under the bottlebrush tree, deep in brambles and thickets and vines. But it is surely he, it must be he: Maxie, My Million.

Sasha, with her little feet, her flexible little body, bravely goes forth into the brush, her sardine plate held high.

"You, little kitten, you come right to me, right now," she commands. I fear Maxie's instinct may be to burrow deeper, hide more urgently, run from her voice. But his nose must catch a whiff of that pungent, tantalizing fish, because Sasha's hand comes back like a policeman's, holding us off, and she freezes, in the manner of a pointer-dog, as Maxie creeps forward through the tangle of twigs.

"Shh," she instructs us. We all watch in wonder, in the dim light of the moon, as Maxie approaches the white paper plate in her hand and bends his head to eat.

Like a snake striking, Sasha grabs him. "Hah!" She holds him by the neck in a triumphant stranglehold.

"I got him! I got him!" she cries.

"Well, good, but now don't kill him," Joanna says, laughing, coming to support Maxie's rear quarters as Sasha dangles him in the air.

"I told you!" she says, turning to me. "I promised you I would find him."

"Yes, you did. And I'm delighted. And I love you," I tell her, picking her up in my arms as she just a moment ago grasped Maxie. "You're wonderful! You're brilliant. I thank you, darling."

"So it *is* a happy new year, isn't it?" Sasha says with satisfaction. "I made it one for all of us."

"Yes, you definitely did."

"So now, can I keep him?"

January 3

Susanna, our youngest daughter, comes home from Berkeley for a brief visit. Her first request is to hold Maxie. It's been so long since there was any liveliness at home, any newness, any variety. A kitten galvanizes a home much as a new baby does; laughter is noticeable again, a certain sweetness, caring, and tenderness become possible; cynicism is banished, hope is renewed. It's possible to be sentimental without embarrassment. Baby talk is allowed. The sense of touch in public is nourished and encouraged.

With our guests gone home, there is more space and more freedom here. Maxie ventures forth without fear of being swept up and devoured by a small, voracious child. Our daughters sprawl on the rug, reaching out to Maxie, sweeping their fingers over his silken fur, holding him above their heads, cooing into his receptive face. They describe his beauty to one another: the white furry seam from his chin down to the bottom of his belly, the intricate concentric circles on his chest, the patterns on his coat that even the most accomplished weaver could not imitate.

Our married daughter, Becky, arrives (she often comes to visit, she and her husband live nearby), and her arrival seems to electrify my sense of wholeness. All three of my children are home again; with J. present, we seem satisfyingly complete, a total entity. A family weightiness envelops us. I think: *My Family.* Maxie's presence enlarges that feeling; we've taken him in, committed our allegiance to him, pledged support and protection. I think we all feel valiant, heroic in some way.

I am gratified to see how happy Susanna is when she plays with Maxie. I feel I have done something right, something of which she can approve and which balances out Korky's final illness two years ago, which in some way I felt was my fault, felt guilty for the fact that life is finite, and finally death will conquer, devastate, and destroy. I wonder if perhaps all mothers feel this guilt when their children recognize that death exists, and no one (not even all-powerful Mother) can do anything about it.

Korky became ill at the end of the year, just before New Year's, when Susanna was home from college for the Christmas break. He had been eating poorly for the last few days and by then was down to a few laps of beaten raw egg; he was breathing heavily, his rib cage heaving.

"We have to take him to the vet," I told Susanna. Becky, who had two cats of her own, and who had arrived at the house to help us assess his condition, agreed.

"He hates it there," Susanna said. "He's very old. If he's going to die, Mom, I think we should let him alone to do it his way."

"But what if something can be done . . .?"

"I don't think so, Mom," she said.

But Becky and I prevailed. We got the cardboard cat-carry box and together Becky and I got Korky inside. Weak as he was, he mewed—a low, sad wailing sound—all the way to the vet's.

⁓

"You have a very sick, very old cat," the young woman vet told us. "He's dehydrated. His breathing is very labored; I suspect he has tumors in his lungs. But to make sure we'll take an x-ray, we'll do a blood workup, we'll keep him overnight and see what we can find out."

"What's the point, Mom?" Susanna whispered to me. "He'll hate being left here. He'll hate all the stuff they'll do to him."

"It's our duty," I said. Becky, in the role of older sister, put her arm around Susanna. I told the vet we'd call her in the morning. My daughters and I stood uncertainly at the door as the vet carried Korky firmly in her arms into their back rooms. Just before we closed the door behind us, we heard an outraged cry: Korky's voice distorted by fear.

∾

"There's nothing we can do," the vet said on the phone in the morning. "There's fluid in his lungs. He's going to get worse as he gets less air. We gave him an enema to help him evacuate, and we injected fluids under his skin to help his dehydration and make him more comfortable. You can take him home, if you like, but, frankly, I would urge you to consider putting him to sleep. You'll save him days, maybe even a week, more or less, of suffering."

"I'll talk to my daughter about it. He's been her special pet for sixteen years. I need to let her decide."

When I hung up the phone, Susanna said, "No. I know what the vet said and my answer is no. If Korky is still able to purr, if he still knows me, I want him here, in his home. I'm not going to give him one day less than he should have."

∾

When we picked Korky up, he reeked of feces. His hindquarters were matted and wet with excrement.

"Oh!" Susanna said. "Look what they did to him. He stinks, and now I can't even hold him. Look at how ashamed he is, he knows how he smells."

"He'll dry off. I'll clean him," I said. "I'll get soap and water and wash his body. Then you can hold him."

"What was the point of our doing this to him?"

I asked myself the same question. Furthermore, though I tried not to consider this, I had the invoice for $250 in my purse for which I had just left a check.

∾

For several days, Korky lay on the rug at the glass door in a little patch of sunshine, his head flat down on the carpet, his nose almost too heavy for him to lift up. If I brought a beaten egg on a flat plate right up to his mouth, he would try to lap once or twice and then turn away.

Susanna sat beside him hour after hour, crooning to him, stroking him, eliciting a faint purr now and then. A few times a day, Susanna carried him to the litter box, but he collapsed in it, seemed to want to sleep in it.

Mainly he used his energy to breathe. He didn't appear to be in pain. Susanna sat vigil at this side, or lay on the rug, her head against his head, reassuring him, loving him.

On his last night, Becky and her husband came to be with us. Her husband and J. sat in the living room, talking softly, while my two daughters and I sat on the bathroom floor, close to Korky. From time to time one of us would caress him carefully. He lay on a soft white shaggy bathrug, for the first time unable to respond to our presence. His gaze was finally inward, directed toward this last powerful experience. He labored to breathe, it took all his concentration. He finally cried out, once, then twice, a little cry of protest or pain or disbelief.

Late that night, we closed the bathroom door very quietly, very softly. Korky's head was down, he did not seem to notice that we were there or that we were saying goodnight.

~

In the morning I rose before dawn, fearing what I would find. I think we all have a terrible resistance to looking upon death. When you know it has made its way into your home despite all your efforts to keep it a safe and secure place, you cringe before its power.

I found Korky dead, his mouth in a snarl, his teeth bared, his eyes open. He was on his side, his paws flung wide, as if he had struck out in a life-and-death struggle, as if he intended to claw an enemy. He lay in his skin, flattened and stiff. He wasn't there. He had gone out. Only the old and discarded shell was left behind.

I went down the hall to Susanna's bedroom and softly opened the door (a liberty I had not taken since she was in grade school). She slept in a great tumble of pillows and quilts. I sat down at the edge of her bed and uncovered her head. I stroked her curly hair.

"Sue," I said. "Korky is gone."

She extracted her arms from under the blankets and reached up to embrace me. "Oh, Mommy," she said. "Oh, no."

$$\sim$$

We called Joanna at school and told her that Korky had died. After we had breakfast, Susanna and Becky chose a place under a great hanging-branched tree at the far end of the yard and J. softened the earth with water before he and Becky took turns digging the grave. Susanna wrapped Korky's body in a woven Mexican jacket that she had loved, and carried him outside, her body shaken by sobs as she laid him softly in the damp earth. She had refused to place him in a box—she was very definite about that.

We marked the grave with a circle of large rocks, and all of us—Becky and her husband, Susanna, J., and I—stood with our arms around one another in the yard Korky had run in and slept in and played in, in the place where he had lived his life for so many years.

Just before we went inside, Susanna laid a strand of ivy on his grave.

February 3

The children have gone back to their respective graduate schools, our company is gone, the extra chairs are stored away, the bedrooms are empty, J. and I are back as we were at the beginning, the two of us alone . . . with the exception of Maxie, who insinuates his silken nose between us at every opportunity.

J. carries from his childhood his mother's admonitions that somehow pets are dirty, unnecessary, and possibly dangerous. My mother communicated these same cautions to me, but once I had a pet (my father brought me home a beagle puppy when I was eleven) I saw at once that the cautions were erroneous, and stood for something more like jealousy, or fear of the child's allegiance being attached to a dumb animal instead of to the proper focus of attention, her parents.

Now, with the house empty, I am free to focus my attention fully and luxuriously on Maxie. It has been so long since I held a child in my lap. Maxie comes to me like a warm rocket, hurtling through the air, biting gently to invite my embrace, then burrowing down, settling and resettling his body, curling, winding, compressing into the perfect position.

Then he begins his harmonious burr, the deep vibration of his purr, the pure buzz of peace. What happens to me at these moments is this: I feel my heart slow at once, my breathing becomes deep, I fall into a meditative trance, staring, letting my hand stroke his silky fur, feeling the baby-bones of his spine—flexible, hidden deep in his structure. I have not felt peace like this for years . . . for centuries! I don't tire of holding him, I think I could sit there for ten hours without becoming restless.

Yet I never keep him there against his will. If he doesn't want to stay, he's gone, simply as that. He's shot away like an arrow, he's down on the rug with his toy, or in the laundry room where he finds the remains of his "shrimp and lobster entree" or he's in his litter box or at the glass door asking to be let out. He can never be seduced to stay against his will.

If I so much as lift him up when he's not of the same mind, he stiffens every muscle, his claws dig in, he twists, he corkscrews away, and then he won't be found unless he wants to be found.

∾

When J. comes home from school he finds me in my desk chair with Maxie asleep in my lap.

"So there you are with your new little boyfriend," he says,

"Are you jealous? Don't you wish you were small enough to curl up in my lap?"

"Maybe my turn will come," he says, smiling. But I know he's glad to see my spirits lifted. I catch him watching me when Maxie climbs up on my desk and places his paws softly on my shoulders. J. hears me laughing when I whirl the killer shoulder-pad on a length of twine and Maxie runs in a circle to catch it. J. appreciates it when I laugh, when I forget the sorrows of the world, the sorrows of my mother. He is willing to have me adore Maxie even if he has no need of this urgent connection himself.

∾

Just when I am feeling comfortable that J. is accepting Maxie, is putting aside his reservations, Maxie destroys the thousand-dollar couch. He is wandering innocently around the living room when suddenly he tears like a bullet into the flesh of the couch, where I see him curved and vibrating in a lunatic fit, lying on his side, his paws convulsing against the wool plaid material. Ripping sounds are in my ears even as I leap to stop him. Too late. The lower left corner is shredded. I see, fluttering into the room, bits of down filling settling to the floor like the feathers of a murdered bird.

Oh no! What now! J. and I shopped for a year before we chose that couch (not so recently: in fact, more than fifteen years ago). But still, it's our treasure, a brown and blue wool plaid with leather trim on the armrests, the edges of the cushions, the back.

Yes, there have already been some small scratches on the leather, which I've concealed with brown shoe wax in the hope that J. would not notice. But this is serious; I examine the rips to see if I may be able to darn them. I wonder if I could distract J. by arranging—for example—a set of fireplace tools just at that corner of the couch. I could tell him I saw it in *Home and Gardens.* Or perhaps I could set up some barriers thrown casually around the couch: an old briefcase, a carton, an old coat, and let J. think it's just clutter I haven't got around to cleaning up.

In any case, I must forestall further damage right now and send Maxie outside. I don't scold him; he's already forgotten the impulse that set him convulsing like a jackhammer.

Like any mother, I know that Maxie must take his baby steps in the real world. Outside are trees that nature has designed for his entertainment. He must make their acquaintance, become familiar with their inviting bark.

When I slide back the door, Maxie doesn't hesitate. He flies into the sunshine, hopping like a bunny, straight for the Chinese elm. I see his muscles taking stock, more so than his brain. Without further consideration, he leaps onto the tree and claws his way up the trunk. Once he is high in its branches, he looks down upon me and meows. This is a terrible cry, almost like the very first cry I heard from behind the grate, from under the house. "What have I done?" he asks me with his beautiful, clever eyes. "Whatever have I done?"

He's framed among the branches; the clusters of leaves take him in and swallow him, blending with his natural camouflage: the swirls and whorls of his mottled fur. He is almost invisible.

He begs me for assistance from deep in his throat.

I murmur some assurances and go into the house. I get busy sopping up the water that has leaked again from the dishwasher. I know that all good mothers let their children learn to solve their own problems.

February 8

We seem to be in a period of crisis. I am a nervous wreck today. It is only midmorning and Maxie has leaped on the oak coffee table and skidded across it like a Dodger trying to steal second base. He has perched on the brick platform of the fireplace and waited, like a kamikaze pilot, to crash-land on top of Big Kitty. If I lock him away in his room in order to get something done, he screams like a temperamental diva, and if I let him out in the house and try to attend to my duties, I have to run into the living room at top speed as soon as I hear the sounds of scraping, tearing, or skidding.

I would let him outside, but I'm leaving the house soon to visit the nursing home, and I'm not confident that he should be out for hours, unwatched, unsummoned. I'm not entirely convinced he knows where his home is, although a friend has told me that "the model is to keep a new kitten in the house for three weeks and then let him out." He has been here considerably longer than that, but maybe he's a slow learner. He doesn't quite seem to understand where the doors to this house are, and that this house is his house.

My heart is pounding, I am dizzy with exhaustion, I feel a hint of the desperation I felt when I was the mother of three little children under five years of age. I'm not built for that anymore—I'm used to peace now, to being able to get something done that I set my mind to doing.

Have I voluntarily and actually committed myself to this agitation for the next twenty years? A baby, at least, has soft fingers and toes. Baby-methods of destruction are even amusing: crayon drawings upon the walls, milk upon the floor, cookies hidden in the clothes hamper.

Maxie's marks of independence are serious; gashes not only on the furniture, but on the window sills, on the pink-toucan wallpaper that J. installed himself in the kitchen. Little tufts of beige yarn have begun appearing in clumps upon the surface of the beige rug. This is hardcore damage; this is serious.

~

Since I have decided I must lock Maxie in his room before I go away, I first lay a hand-crocheted shawl on the washing machine to improve his cushion, then I line up a few of his toys—a plastic turtle I found in the street, a golf ball, a furry stuffed bunny, two clothespins attached to some yarn—and I assure him I will be back soon, this is not punishment, this is rest-time, and yes, I promise I will be back with a surprise for him soon.

He cocks his little head toward me, his eyes seeking my face, his pink nose a silent valentine. He's on the washer now, chest high to me, so I hug him, and he places one paw gently on my chest, his trademark of tenderness, and this time a soft farewell.

My sister, B., calls me to discuss the logistics of visiting our mother. She and I have agreed that it's better to go together, more fun for us, less strain (we spell each other in arguing with our mother, or running interference with requests to the nurses' station), but we see the sense of going separately, staggering our visits so that we not only appear to visit more often, but actually do check up on our mother's condition more often.

My sister tells me she's read of a group called CAPS (Children of Aging Parents) that meets at the local Jewish Center, and would I like to go with her? We are, after all, children of an aging parent. In fact, she reminds me, we ourselves are aging children of an aging parent and we are so old, she says, that our children should also go to this meeting. That's how it is with my sister: she survives by making jokes. She claims it's hard to cry when you're laughing.

We agree that today will be my day to visit. Tomorrow will be her day. Someday (we both think it) it will be no one's day, it will be all over. But not yet.

~

I find my mother as always, motionless, in the same space of the universe she now occupies all the time. "This bed is my home now," she told me once. "I will live here till I die."

"Mom," I whisper. She isn't asleep. I wait for her to respond. I breathe with difficulty here, the air in the nursing home feels different in my lungs. The room itself inspires awe in me, I feel myself in the presence of a great, inescapable force. My mother turns her head slowly toward the doorway, in my direction, and murmurs, "You're just in time."

Indeed: I am "in time"—I still wander carelessly in it, free to come and go, to choose my direction and my purpose, to speed through it, or to let it pass slowly through me. She always greets me this way—saying that I'm just in time.

"In time for what?" I ask her. We don't bother with formal greeting now; she likes to get right on to business.

"I think someone has stolen one of my robes. Open that closet and count my robes. See if there are seven." The wheelchair is blocking the closet. She asks me to do this every time I come. Of course no one has stolen her robes; they all have her name in thick black marker-pen written on the collars, I personally wrote her name on each and every robe.

I oblige her, anyway. It also gives me something to do. I wheel away the wheelchair, I open the closet, I count: the aqua robe, the blue flowered robe, the pink satin robe, the red quilted robe, the white terrycloth robe, robe after robe, the wardrobe of royalty is here.

"They steal anything that isn't nailed down," my mother says, one of her refrains.

I pull up an orange plastic chair and sit down to begin the visit. By the time I leave I will be breathless with talking hard, talking loud, talking fast. I feel as if I ought to compress my talking, accordion shape, so my mother can unfold it, let it out slowly when I am gone, listen to the sound of my voice even when I have fled, rushed away to be free.

February 10

B. is seven years younger than I am, but recently we have come to feel we are the same age. When I was away in college and she was still at home, I used to write her letters of advice about how to succeed in school, how to handle our parents, and how to fall in love. Now I often call her for advice. We have come a long way together, we are both grown-up women.

We have conferred and decided to go the CAPS meeting to see what we can learn about being "children of aging parents." B. picks me up in her car and together we drive to the Jewish Center. There are two female "facilitators" at the meeting, and eight visitors who sit in a circle, holding Styrofoam cups of tea, introducing themselves. We all admit that we're baffled to be here, identifying ourselves as (aging) children of very aged parents.

Except for one man, who says he has come to learn about "resources" in the community, the rest of us are women. We give a brief explanation of our problems: for most of the others the complaint has to do with time, money, exhaustion. Either their elders are still living alone and are in constant states of emergency, or are living at home with them, making demands that would tax the wisest, most patient, most loving child.

The case histories have amazing similarities. B. and I begin to throw each other glances. Oddly, we smile at each other. I think we are both feeling grateful that we are further along in this journey of caring for our mother than the others are: our mother, at least, is in a nursing home, and has 24-hour care. She is not alone, with only a phone line to us for contact, and we on call day and night at the other end. We have already passed through that period (five years!) during which she phoned us at early hours of the morning, in panic, feeling dizzy or lonely or truly ill, having just fallen, or had a nosebleed, or lost her memory for several minutes. We are through with those wild rides to her side, imagining that we will find her dead on the floor. We are through with those endless trips to doctors, holding our tottering mother on our arm, getting the medicines she needed, taking her for minor surgery, listening for hours on the phone to her needs and fears.

Now there is no phone at her side. Even if there were, she couldn't hold it to her ear. If she is ill and needs a doctor, he is called to the nursing home, and if there is truly an emergency, she is transported by ambulance to the hospital.

B. and I, who are out of the loop, look at each other feeling grateful, and feeling luckier, somehow, than the others who are telling their sad tales.

And then, I sneeze. I sneeze and fumble for a tissue and don't find one, and sneeze again and reach blindly toward B., waving my arm at her to indicate that I need a tissue. As she starts to look in her purse, she sneezes, too! She looks up at me, her nose dripping, and I look at her, mine dripping, and we begin to laugh.

The trouble is, we are laughers, and this is one of those moments. As children we just had to look at one another, especially at serious moments, and we would burst out laughing. We'd laugh under our covers at night till our father had to come and quiet us. We'd laugh at the dinner table at the sight of some particularly weird food my mother had cooked, or at how the Jell-O shimmered on the spoon, or how the chicken leg lay on the plate. We'd burst into giggles at any ceremony or speech we had to attend.

Now hardly children anymore, in a serious meeting, during which people are pouring out their miseries (one woman is just in the process of describing how her mother falls whenever she tries to walk to the bathroom herself), my sister and I crack up. We have no self-control, not even a semblance of adult maturity. We have sneezed and now we think it's the funniest thing that has ever happened on earth. We double over in our chairs, trying not to laugh out loud, but we are beyond help.

The facilitators, two kind women, look at us with understanding, but not with much amusement. They pause in their discussion, no doubt thinking that we will now get hold of ourselves and gain control, but their glance sets us off again, we grab hands between our chairs, and a new explosion of laughter shakes our shoulders.

This is unreal. We still haven't got tissues, our noses are running, our eyes are tearing with laughter, we are going crazy, new gales of laughter cascading down upon us like an avalanche. And now I also have to go to the bathroom.

I stand up, and stagger toward the kitchen of the meeting room, and my sister follows behind me. We are laughing so hard we can barely walk. I get a glimpse of the others in the circle, staring at us with disbelief. The woman who has been telling her sad tale appears outraged.

It's beyond us though—we have been seized by some force that shakes the laughter out of us till it turns to tears. My sister and I, doubled over, lean against the sink, laughing and crying, now mainly crying, each trying to catch our breath, trying to stop this fit. She tears a paper towel from the roller and hands it to me, and I take one look at the little ducks on it and start on a new roar of laughter. Then we are both wiping our faces and our eyes and our noses with stiff paper toweling with little ducks on it. Nothing has ever seemed funnier.

My sister pulls open a drawer in the kitchen and pulls out a corkscrew and brandishes it at me. She is trying to threaten me into silence.

This is hopeless. We are not children of aging parents, we seem to be lunatics of aging parents, we have lost it. B. finally runs back to the meeting room and retrieves our purses, blurting out some kind of apology, and then comes back to the kitchen, takes my hand and drags me out through a back door to the parking lot. She gets us into her car, turns on the motor, and burns rubber.

She drops me off at my door and waves me out without speaking. I am almost too weak to walk! I struggle up the steps and ring the bell, too exhausted to find my key.

J. opens the door to see me wet-faced and bedraggled on the doorstep. "It must have been quite a meeting," he says. "Want to tell me about it?"

February 11

A great commotion of crows calls me out to the pool deck. Waves of them are blackening the sky, they call to and fro to one another, landing on trees up and down the street. They rattle the pecan tree above me and I look up. Through its winter-bare branches I see an enormous kestrel, staring down with predatory eyes, its shoulders hunched, its curved beak pointing directly down at me. No wonder the crows are in wild flight—I feel the threat myself.

I retreat into the house and hunt for Maxie, who is sleepily curled in a cave he's discovered between the piano and the wall. How little he knows of the dangers that await him.

～

When I am sure the kestrel is gone, I cautiously let Maxie out into the yard, watching the skies. Carefree as a baby, he heads for the yew tree and dives into it, forgetting all the troubles he has with trees and how worried he gets once he's at the top of one.

Without a thought, he claws his way into its dense growth. The tree leans against the garage wall, the same tree that Big Kitty hid in for a day when he was a tiny kitten. I remember Kitty's terrified face looking out; Maxie, once he's deep inside the dense foliage, has a different expression, more determined: he wears an "I'll take the challenge" look. And when, after a half hour of shaking the tree loose of an avalanche of dead leaves, he meows in distress, I offer to help him out. But the instant I part the branches and extend my hand to him, he whacks at my hand, claws extended: *go away, Mommy, let me do it myself.*

What he finally does is travel upward till he finds himself on the roof of the garage. One glance around seems to tell him what he wants to know: this is not a world he is keen to explore just now. In two minutes flat, he has nose-dived back through the tree to dry land. He begs to come in and take a perch on the living room couch, where the height factor is more acceptable. He doesn't seem to worry about anything beyond the moment. I feel I should learn from him.

≈

It's true that his spirit enlarges mine. His willingness to take risks, to explore, to do it on his own, are not metaphors for living, but are *living.* Of course, he's an animal; he can't calculate risks beyond the simplest ones: will I survive this? Survive is what he definitely wants to do, and fiercely. But on his own terms.

≈

I wonder if I should let him out into a world where a kestrel may watch from a tree. Should I leave him out at night with the sound of coyotes howling in the nearby canyons? And what of the raccoons who make their way across the roof of the house on some predetermined path, stopping to eat the cat food, to drink of the pool water (once to defecate in the pool).

Maxie knows only what he discovers about wilderness, what he can learn from the scents and sounds of it; I know it by reading about predators, by warnings in the newspaper about coyotes coming down from the hills to seek water and food. I know it too by the blood-curdling cries of coyotes in the night, those yipping screams, those chilling howls of hunger and threat.

≈

As I write this Maxie is lying across my arms; the computer is on my lap, and with each keystroke, I see his head and body vibrate. He is comforted by the rhythm, by the warmth of my chest, by the reassurance that I am here. And in turn I am moved by the trusting weight of his warm, responsive body.

February 14

At night there is an electrical storm so wild that hailstones big as marbles crash down upon the patio. Maxie, whose hair stands on end if I so much as turn on the hairdryer, is oddly peaceful at the onslaught of lightning bolts and crashing thunder. He lies relaxed, but alert, on the dry side of the sliding glass door, and watches nature's display with the merest interest.

Big Kitty has gone to sleep on top of my down comforter on the king-size bed, which is off-limits to him. I pretend I don't know he's there, not having the energy for the confrontation. Besides, he and I both know who's getting the lion's share of attention. As dense as he seems, he knows. Big Kitty is offended if not seriously depressed.

As the rain pours down, I think of how cozy the house seems. For dinner I am baking chicken basted with barbecue sauce, and my breadmaker is groaning through the kneading cycle. The sound of the hail on the skylight in the kitchen is rhythmic and fierce; but we are safe, warm, dry inside, all of us together. I see a bird on the window sill and feel sorry I can't bring the entire animal world inside for a few hours. We could be a peaceable kingdom here, in harmony, out of the rain and wind, in the warmth of the firelight.

Maxie trots into the kitchen; he smells chicken, perhaps. But no, he wants my company. Because, as I sit down to peel some potatoes, he materializes in my lap. He doesn't seem to travel there, but he arrives. I see his eyes looking up, and then he's simply there, light as a feather. There is no sense of energy spent in his leap, no gasp of effort, no sound of takeoff; in one instant he's down below, in the next, he's lightly pressed against me, placing his delicate paw on my shoulder, and then moving it upward, to caress my face. No claws are in evidence, his footpads on my skin are like powder puffs.

I let him touch my face; I stroke his cheek. He turns to lick my fingers, one at a time.

J., who is reading the paper at the table, cannot fail to notice this tender exchange. He is expressionless; is he jealous? Shall I put Maxie in his lap? But I know too well the changes of weather in Maxie's soul; he could, without any provocation, unsheathe his claws, dig in, thrash around, jump off. One who is experienced can read the changes in his muscles like a blind person must feel the dots of the Braille alphabet. The tiniest tensing brings a new meaning to the story. J. is not schooled in this discipline. He does not seem an eager student at the moment, either.

"Look how adorable Maxie is," I say to J., and realize this is not going to win him over. He looks even lonelier, more rejected, than Big Kitty. "Not as adorable as you, though," I add, peeling the last of the potatoes and wiping my hands on the dishcloth. "This storm is wild. Dinner won't be ready for a couple of hours. Why don't we get under the covers for a while?"

≈

In the morning, the world is puddled and glistening, but drying out. Maxie tears through the house like a whirling dervish; a dash to the glass door, a dash across the bricks of the fireplace, a leap onto the edge of the couch, a skid across the coffee table, a brief wrestle with his stuffed fluffy troll on the rug, a smashing dash against the scratching post and a rebound against the bookcase. What is going on?

"Out?" I ask, and he trots in relief toward the door, flinging his nose straight against it until he's whacked to a sudden stop. I slide the door open. Then out! Out! Into the fragrant, washed air of morning. He can't contain himself. He makes for the pepper tree, but claws himself up only about a foot and gives it up. Then he attacks the yew tree, but remembers he's been there—it's too dense, its branches are thin, they make for poor footing. Maxie backtracks toward the door, where (as if he meant to all the time) he chooses the beginner's tree—the little decorative bush, not more than five feet tall, loosely packed in its interior, a mini-challenge for an inexperienced climber, but giving the appearance of a real tree. He saves face and climbs clear up to the top of it. I laugh and close the door. Let him get down on his own. Let him gain confidence and grow up to be a strong, brave boy.

February 17

Flea bites dot my belly this morning. Fleas are not supposed to thrive in wintertime. Except, I suppose, in California. The damage caused by Maxie increases each day. I find myself giving up to it; so what if the furniture is covered with towels, old coats, and piles of books, if fleas infest the rugs, if the kitchen smells each morning of litter fumes? There is a greater good at stake here.

After dinner I give Maxie a trout tail, tender with flakes of fish flesh. He is shivering with the discovery of such an unexpected ecstasy.

A fury then engulfs him: fish-energy! He tears in his destructive pattern from one side of the living room to the other and back, stopping briefly to rip at the couch, then the chair, then dig his claws into the rug. I rush for the water-pistol, having just read in a cat book about its efficacy (especially if the kitten thinks some unidentifiable force, not me, has squirted him).

But I don't like guns, even a 79-cent toy, and give it up after one squirt. His wildness is not rational, not intentional, not logical, and, surely, he is not "bad." In fact, he is my model for pure joy, for acting on impulse, for the pleasure of making instantaneous choice. I watch him the way I used to watch my babies, in thrall, in awe, in love. But there's a new dimension.

I used to think, somehow, that I made my babies, had participated psychically and physically in their production, while with Maxie I know that I didn't make him at all, did not contribute. This does not separate me from him, but, to the contrary, binds me to him. I feel he was made like me, by the forces of the universe, by accident, perhaps (or by design), but we are both full of pounding life, energy, intelligence, hope. We seek contact, we seek adventure, we seek communion.

Amazing: to deduce all this from one little kitten.

~

We see an animal in the yard: Maxie sees him first, through the glass of the door. It's huge, gray, nosing about Big Kitty's food dish. Could it be one of those possums, with a dirty rat's tail, a dumb stare, close-set eyes? Or even a raccoon, sly, wily, alert for danger? But no—this is a huge, striped gray cat, bold and indifferent, standing just outside the door. Maxie is confused; if it's Big Kitty (and I think he believes it is), he wants to go out and play, tease, irritate.

But how can I inform him that this is a Total Stranger? And therefore dangerous.

I open the sliding glass door just a crack; Maxie's nose goes into it, his hindquarters shivering like a hunting dog's waiting for release to the fox hunt.

The stranger-cat hisses, hunches his back, enlarges like a balloon. Maxie withdraws his nose. He looks up at me with astonishment. Danger? Evil? On his own back step?

The first of many lessons of life, I think to myself, as I close the door firmly, scoop him up, reassure him, carry him back into warmth and safety.

February 18

Since my cat book tells me orange peels are repellent to cats, I have placed bowls of orange peels beside the leather couch and the matching chair. Over the leather ottoman I spread a red sleeping bag for protection, and I also hang sheets of tinfoil on the lower third of the drapes. Balloons, says my cat book, will work also; when the cat jumps up, the balloons will pop, and traumatize him for life.

I am such a busy little person, busy racing in with cat treats when Maxie uses the scratching post (he doesn't care much for the cat treats—I have to force them in between his teeth as if I were giving him medicine!)—busy shoving orange peels into place, busy devising how to protect one place when I discover that he has just found a new area to destroy.

My cat book authors say if damage gets too bad, I can clip the tips of his claws. Are they kidding me? Get Maxie in a choke hold, wear elbow-high leather gloves as if I were training a falcon? Clip not one, but ten claws? Let's be realistic. "If you happen to clip the quick of his nail, your cat will howl and bleed rather profusely. Press the bleeding claw with a cotton ball. It is not certain your cat will allow you to continue with the grooming process."

No, indeed, I can understand why it would not be certain. Still, it's worth a try, isn't it?

~

I place Maxie on a pillow on my lap; a soft Chopin impromptu is playing on my tape player. I distract him by typing for a while on my laptop computer. He dozes, pacified by the tap of the keys just at the tip of his ears. We have done this before and he is trusting. He sighs, snuggles closer, seems to go to sleep. When I think the moment is upon us, I gently reach for the nail-clippers, gently take his limp paw in my fingers, gently press on a paw-pad to eject his claw. Then, suddenly, I snip!

Maxie is out of my lap like a lightning bolt.

Ah well, we'll deal with this another time.

February 20

The break in the rain has come just in time for me to pop Maxie into the Cat Taxi and take him to the Veterinary Outreach Clinic, which is a cut-rate operation carried on in the parking lots of various pet stores. This time, my second such venture with Maxie, I know I'm not going to get him into the carrier face first, pushing and shoving while he digs his claws onto any surface, including my thighs, to resist. This time I know the trick; turn the carrier on end and lower him, feet first.

It works like a charm, until the instant he realizes he's in a cage. From deep in his throat, he emits the most hideous howl. It sounds like nothing else on earth. I think it means he thinks he's going to die. The desperation and powerful grief in his voice chill my soul.

I calm him the best I can, telling him that it won't hurt, that it's for his own good, that he'll be happy in the long run. As I carry him in his case to the car, he flings himself from one side to the other. I place the Pet Taxi on the back seat and make soothing noises. As we drive along (Dvorak on the tape player) he cries more softly, the sounds getting weaker, pitiful bleats of fear and protestation.

At the designated parking lot there's a long line of dogs and cats, accompanied by owners with their checkbooks out and at the ready. The rule is that you tell an attendant what shots you need, you write your check, you are then given poker chips of varying colors to indicate vaccinations you've just purchased, and then your pet is taken away for his treatment.

The dogs are hefted, one by one, onto a card table, while the cats are taken into a little trailer for their shots.

The young man who has me fill out an application on the clipboard asks me how old Maxie is.

"I'm not sure, maybe you can tell me. I'd also like to know at what age he needs to be altered."

"When his testicles come down," he says. The boy looks to be about twenty, handsome, with intelligent eyes.

"How would I know when that is?"

"Well, you feel," he says. "If they're down, he's ready."

Seeing my puzzled look, he feels for Maxie's testicles and apparently discovers them. He looks at me, as if he will offer me a chance to feel them, too, but he sees what's in my face.

"He's ready," he says. "Any time now."

I smile at him, thankful that he has not asked me to verify his findings. The line moves up. The vet turns out to be a shining blonde young woman, who says in surprise as she takes Maxie by the scruff of the neck, "Well! It looks like you've got yourself a purebred Manx."

"Really?" I say. "Is he? Purebred?"

"He has all the standard features—the round eyes, rounded back, the stumpy tail, long hind legs. Manx cats make wonderful pets, almost like dogs. They adore their owners. He's very valuable."

"I know, he's very valuable to me."

"He's worth quite a bit, also, in dollars."

When I tell the vet how I discovered him (how he was a giveaway, even a throwaway), she says, "How lucky you are."

Maxie gets his shots, not feeling at all lucky. I tell him I know how it is; I hate doctor visits, too.

March 4

My mother is in the hospital again. Her cage, at some point, becomes more than unbearable to her so that she prefers action, any action, to the status quo. Thus she agitates till the mechanism starts moving, even if it's toward destruction. Her complaint in the summer, whose cause was relatively harmless, brought ruin upon her, and who knows what this complaint will bring down.

An aide calls from the nursing home to say my mother is being taken by ambulance and will be at the hospital in twenty minutes.

"Are you calling to ask my permission?" I say.

"No. We just have to notify the family."

~

On the way to the hospital I stop at the thrift shop and look through a box of stuffed animals. I burrow into a cave of teddy bears, monkeys, whales, dogs, fish, snakes, bunnies, alligators, and mice. It's a big, deep cardboard box, and I wonder how I could possibly join the animals there, live in this fluffy kingdom, and not face what I have to face today. Some of the animals squeak, some moo, some tinkle with silver bells.

I choose for Maxie a big yellow parrot wearing a Hawaiian grass skirt; when squeezed, it makes a little desperate cry like a bird, perhaps, being caught by a big cat. I also buy him a little striped snake, filled with tiny dried beans. Perhaps this toy is meant to resemble a rattlesnake; it should tap into Maxie's primitive instincts, especially if I dip it in catnip.

~

They have my mother on a gurney in the emergency room; she has to be evaluated before they know what is to be done with her. Her complaint: stomach pain in the vicinity of her feeding tube. Terrible pain. "I've never had pain like this before." I'm kind enough not to tell her that she says that every time, about every pain. I sit beside her. Doctors are visible going into curtained cubicles; the bottoms of their legs can be seen, their shoes. I watch them step about in the steps of The Emergency Room Dance, doing what they do, exercising those dark secrets that doctors keep, those life-saving secrets.

"When are they coming to see me?" my mother demands.

"After they treat the real emergencies," I say.

"And I'm not one of them?"

"You're not dying this minute, Mom."

Why am I so unkind? She is dying this minute, minute by minute. As am I.

Finally a doctor comes our way. He's not young, he might be seventy.

"And what can we do for you today?" he says to both of us.

My mother says, "I'm no good for anything."

"She hates getting old," I tell him.

"Tell me about it," he says, smiling kindly. "So what else is new?"

March 5

I leave Maxie asleep on my desk chair (alone at home, with the entire house at his disposal for the first time) and set out for the hospital. My mother has been admitted with a diagnosis of an infected feeding tube wound; from her voice on the phone she sounds triumphant. *See, I'm sick enough for the hospital again. I told you so!*

She doesn't remember what her last trip to the hospital provided her with—a stroke and a broken hip. She only remembers her refrain: "I don't care what they do to me; I can't live with this pain." There has always been an unbearable pain somewhere in her body that can't be lived with. A headache, a stiff neck, an ingrown toenail, a sprained finger—but always intolerable, exquisite, excruciating.

How many times I have said to her: "Mom, you've had so many pains in your life. Let's not rush off to the doctor so fast. Be a little patient."

"But never a pain like this," has been her refrain. *"Never* like this."

~

I breathe shallowly in the hospital, as if I can keep the militant organisms just outside my vulnerable places. I look into rooms as I pass along the hall, seeing examples of the varieties of illness and pain that are possible in this universe.

I see human beings like me hooked to machines, or sleeping, or watching soap operas; all of them in a place in the script of life where I am not, at this particular moment.

In one room I see a young woman in a black sweater and pants stretched out, full length, lying close against a patient. I don't know if the patient is a man or a woman, an old person or a child, a sister, or lover, or mother to the person who is in the embrace. But what is etched into my mind is the contrast of the black figure pressed against the white sheets covering the person who is destined to spend this day (and God knows how many more) in the hospital.

On I walk. I am in a kind of trance, forgetting why I am walking here. When I see my mother's face in a bed, I am actually startled.

"Well," she says. "Look who's here." Her little alert face peers over her sheets.

"And look who's here," I say to her. We are like two tourists meeting on the Bridge of Sighs.

"I didn't expect *you* today," she says, as if there are endless possibilities, endless days.

"Who did you expect? The Queen of England?"

A nurse comes in and my mother says at once, "Oh, did you want me?" Her implication is that if someone wants her she can be had at once; I am no impediment. She confirms this. "This is only my daughter," she says. And to me she adds, "This is Debbie, an absolutely charming girl."

So much for that. But I know how she tends to court those in authority, how powerless she feels, not only in her present position, but in the way she has felt all her life.

She has often recounted to me the abuses of the aides at the nursing home, but never tells me their names since she fears I will report them. "They would just get even with me. And if they were fired, they might come to get me, to kill me. They would make my life a living hell."

Sometimes I am reassured by this comment; maybe it proves that in fact her life isn't *already* a living hell.

The nurse is dropping off a lunch tray. My mother has had her feeding tube disconnected while the infection is being treated, and therefore, she must eat by mouth. She can do it; she simply has chosen to give up eating, along with walking. It's easier, she can't be bothered. Occasionally, in the months since she surrendered herself entirely to the feeding tube, she will take some chocolate ice cream for what the dietitian calls "oral gratification."

I tell the nurse I will feed her, and my mother says, "Oh no, your arm will get tired. You'll get food on your nice dress. Let the nurse do it."

Does she really prefer the nurse to me, or does she want her money's worth, the service to which she's entitled? One of the reasons she says she gave up eating in the nursing home was because the aides would "jam it down my throat, let it drip down my chin. They were always in a hurry. So let the tube keep me alive, who cares if I eat or not?"

I tell the nurse I'll be happy to feed her. I tuck a towel under her chin like a bib . . . and I begin.

She is actually hungry, and the shimmering squares of yellow Jell-O look delicious, even to me. There's chicken broth, there's apple juice, there's tea, and an orange Popsicle. I see her enjoyment and I feel proud, as if she's my baby having her first solid food.

~

After lunch, she tells me a story of her waking dream. "I opened my eyes from a deep sleep, and I was in a storeroom," she says. "I thought they had put me in a storage area. There were cartons and boxes all around. It was dark. I was frightened and alone. A man came in wearing a uniform. I thought he would harm me, or injure me, or rape me. I said 'Who are you?' and he said he was a nurse. 'Why am I in a storage room with all these boxes?' I said, and he answered, 'You're in a hospital and I'm a nurse. What you see isn't a box up there, it's the television, and just under it, that square shape, that's the sink. And over here is the paper towel holder, it looks like a box. And over there is the box for dangerous waste, that red metal thing on the wall. You're not in a storeroom.'"

"So did you feel better then?"

I am imagining her fear—a fear of being put in a box, of being boxed in, and forgotten. A fear, perhaps, of the coffin.

"I didn't feel better. I thought he would harm me, hurt me, rape me."

We look at each other. Even if she is eighty-five, my mother is still female, still sexual. (Though when we discussed her having to be bathed at the nursing home by a male attendant, she once said to me, "What does it matter? I'm not a woman anymore . . . I'm nothing now.")

"No one will rape you, Mom, I promise."

"I suppose it wouldn't be the worst thing."

Suddenly, I remember a scene in the movie *All That Jazz,* in which the hero, who has had a heart attack, wanders through the halls of the hospital and enters the room of an old woman. There, he kisses her passionately on the lips. She embraces him in return. I recognize that the worst thing is to be nothing. That is what this struggle to stay alive and human is all about.

March 9

My mother is being discharged from the hospital today. After a battery of exhausting tests—an endoscopy, an upper GI series, a barium enema, a colonoscopy—"they" decided she needed her feeding tube replaced. A specialist was consulted; a surgeon has already performed the surgery—which took place uneventfully except for one small problem. As my mother was being transferred from the gurney to the operating table, the side of the gurney was lowered onto her arm. A nurse calls me from my mother's bedside at the hospital: "Although your mother is doing just fine, we're required to report this incident to you. We've already x-rayed her arm—nothing is broken, although she says her arm is a little sore. She'll be going back to the nursing home in just a little while—the ambulance has already been called. Would you like to talk to her?"

"I can't hold the phone!" I hear my mother moan.

"I'll hold it for you," says the nurse.

I hear heavy breathing. My mother's breathless voice seems to come from a distance. She is panting. "I think they broke my arm. And the pain! They let you lie here like a dog. I can't talk anymore."

"Mom—I'll see you at the nursing home in a little while. Okay, Mom?" I listen for an answer but there is silence. I have the sense she's dropped the phone on the bed, unable to hang it up. I feel voyeuristic, listening to what must be her heavy breathing, the breathing of pain. Suddenly she bursts out with her hopeless wish, her prayer, her mantra.

"I wish I were dead," she sobs with such fervor that a shiver passes through me. "I wish I were dead." *(I-wish-I-were* is one phrase, with a pause, and then the word: *dead.)* Unable to hang up, I hang on, I listen, my heart nearly stopping, and hear her say, "Oh what should I do with this PAIN?" Then: suddenly, she says my name. She is calling me, in desperation, and I'm not there, I'm gone, I was supposed to have hung up. But I'm summoned.

"Ma! Ma!" I yell into the phone. "I'm here, can you hear me?" But she's too far away, floating in the river of morphine—she can't discern that I am still with her. I hang up, cry out with a few bursts of tears, and blindly make myself some lunch.

~

Pickled herring in sour cream, bread and butter and coffee. Even as I eat, men in uniform are transporting her through the hallways and elevators of the hospital, are loading her into an ambulance. ("Your mother will be Medevaced," the discharge planner had told me on the phone. *Medevac* sounds like war to me.)

I drink my coffee and realize how separate we are: I have my life, she has hers. She's in her own little boat on her own little river, navigating her own rapids. I look on from the shore, separate and destined to fulfill a fate entirely different from hers. I don't have to get into her boat, I can't get into it. I don't even have to stand there on the bank and watch it drift, oarless, into the sunset. Or so I tell myself.

On my way to the nursing home, I stop off at The Bargain Box. I have only twenty-five minutes in the thrift shop before it closes, so I rush, I examine the jewelry counter, I run to the Women's Two-Piece Outfits, I paw through Women's Dresses, I flip the hangers in Women's Sportswear. I see nothing that will fill the void in me; today is not a shopping day.

~

My mother is back in the nursing home, but this time her bed is in the Medicare wing where "acute care" is dispensed. Her head is on a pillow, her paralyzed hand propped on another pillow, her white hair brushed back over her forehead.

"Mother," I say, and she says, "Well, I didn't expect you today." She barely seems to know she's been away.

But at once I see all the new problems created by her brief absence. The little TV is on the wrong side of the bed where she can't reach it. The feeding tube is not connected (it's not even in the room!) so she isn't getting any fluid or nourishment, her head is not raised, her foot cradle is not in place to keep the blanket from resting heavily on her toes.

I set about getting things right. I speak to the nurses, to the maintenance men. ("We have to have the TV shackled," my mother tells me, "so no one steals it." She actually uses the word *shackled*.) "And my clothes," she says, "I want you to count my robes and be sure to take some home. If they see I have this many, they'll steal them."

"You're better off having them here, Mom," I say. "I mean, I don't need them, and you might want to have them. When the weather gets warm, you'll need the thin ones."

She begins to name the robes again, calling them out like the names of her children: "I have the blue flowered and the pink satin and the red quilted and—take home that thick terrycloth one, it's too heavy for me."

We hear a moan from the next bed. My mother glances over and makes a face. She discounts the human being there—if anything, the person will only prove an annoyance to her. She's learned, over the succession of many roommates, that the best roommate is catatonic, the next best is mobile and will wheel herself out in the morning and stay out all day. The worst are those that "eat like a horse" and watch TV "from morning to night, usually soap operas and Jesus programs."

I don't have time now to inquire into the condition and status of the new roommate. I simply do all that I have to do to get my mother reinstated in her place.

I ask the nurses to hurry with the pain medication. I ask for a razor, and shave the four long whiskers on my mother's chin. I give my mother my lip balm for her chapped lips. I wear myself out jumping around.

"What am I keeping you from?" my mother asks. She seems to have forgotten her recent trauma in the hospital. She seems to sense my exhaustion, my readiness to leave.

"I have to cook my husband dinner," I say, the good wife, the willing slave.

"I love you," my mother says. "Tell him I love him, too," my mother adds.

We look at each other. We never know when she will finally have her wish and truly die, so we enact our farewells at every meeting. Today I feel they are weighted with hollowness. Today the words are merely part of our script.

"Goodbye, Mom. I'll be back soon."

March 12

Maxie lets me touch his private parts, his tiny sharp teeth, the tender center of his belly, the soft pads of his paws. He lets me eject his claws by pressure on the bottom of his feet, he lets me turn his ears inside out. The little triangle of his head seduces me, that tiny handful of brain and will and need and energy. "His eyes are so expressive," my mother says when I visit her today and show her some pictures of the kitten. "My dog never had such expressive eyes."

I touch my mother as freely as I touch the cat. I check to see if her toe might be getting gangrenous again, I take the razor from her drawer and shave off the tiny new growth of the whiskers on her chin, I pull back the sheets and examine her incisions, two of them, both still held together by metal staples on either side of the hole from which the feeding tube extrudes.

I look at the soft white belly I lived in for a time, and below, the even more private place that I came out of, now just another neutral body part, no more, no less.

How I know my mother's parts. Every finger, the smoothness of her shoulders, the delicacy of her spine, the wide soft spread of her hips, and her beautiful, shapely legs. The bunions on her feet are not graceful, but they are hidden.

She has been out of the hospital three days and is still in the Medicare unit. The nurses all know her; she has been in this wing many times, after her femoral bypass surgery (to correct blood flow to her lower leg, to try to save the toe that became gangrenous), after her stroke and broken hip (how hard the therapists tried to get her to walk again, but she refused to fight).

There is one special nurse my mother loves; Leroy from South Africa, who calls her Jessie, not Yessie (as do the Mexican aides), and touches her whenever he comes by, with a strong, hard grasp. When she says, as she does today, "I don't want any more of this" (life, is what she means), he says, "You stay, Jessie, you stay as long as you can and take what is given. Some are only given one year, some three years, and you, you are given eighty-five years. So be thankful. And when you're called, you'll go peacefully, but not before that. You hear me?" Even I hear him, feel fatalistic in his presence, feel the power of whatever it is he believes.

My mother says to me when he leaves, "I'm glad you came, I have a lot to tell you," and she begins by saying, "See that big heavy bottle of Gevity, that's what keeps me alive. Someone left it upside-down in my kitchen, and I had to carry it somewhere and I couldn't lift it, so I needed a big strong man, so who did I call, I called Will." I pull my chair closer and look at her face carefully. Will is my father, dead now for twenty-eight years.

My mother says, "I called, 'WILL! WILL!' and he didn't come and I said to myself 'Why isn't he coming!' and then I remembered: he can't come, why am I calling him, he's dead! He's dead!"

Tears roll down my mother's cheeks. She has just lost my father again, here, now, at this moment while I sit beside her.

I take her hand, but she doesn't respond. Down the hall I hear the cries of other patients, "Help me! Help me. I can't do anything for myself." It's like a chorus from hell here, in every room someone is ringing the bell, or crying out, or begging for help or sleeping his way toward eternity.

Sometimes I do not have the heart for these visits. Just when I think I've got it under control, have hardened my heart suffi- ciently, have a grasp of the philosophical realities of all this living and dying, just when I think I've managed to get some balance regarding the Basic Rules of Life, I suffer a failure of nerve. I can't find a notion in all of heaven or hell why the world was designed this way—I simply don't know why we live, why we love, and why we die.

March 14

There is always a worry that once I let Maxie outside, he may not come home. My confidence in him is greater than it was, but there's always that hollow falling away of my breath, the thump of fear, after I call his name from the back door and—after an interval—he does not come.

As a child, I was impressed by the book *The Princess and the Goblin*, in which the young heroine can always find her way back to the room from which she sets out on an adventure by wearing a ring that is attached to an invisible string. I would like to be able to spool Maxie back to me, winding him up to my very finger. But in life, such certainties are not guaranteed.

The times Maxie *does* appear to my summons, this is what I see: he comes rapidly around a corner of the yard and perches on the circle of rocks that cover Korky's grave. He sits on the grave, looking at me across the wide plain of the back yard, ears pointed, tiny haunches tucked neatly under him, eyes wide. And then, fast as a cheetah, he races toward me with a speed that suggests enormous longing, he leaps into the house through the door I hold open with an eagerness that suggests pent-up passion, and I fall on him with a cry of joy.

Separations and reunions of operatic proportions occur regularly at this back door. I sweep him into my arms and he nuzzles under my chin. We coo and purr at one another, I call him "my little sweetheart baby."

J. sometimes looks up from his newspaper at my squeals of joy, at my laughter, at my cooing, at my dancing around the room with Maxie in my arms, at my singing . . . and smiles at us. Sometimes I thrust Maxie under his nose, saying, "Say hello, Maxie, say hello," and J. will touch the tip of Maxie's nose with one finger and say, "Hi, Maxie."

~

I keep making Maxie new collars. At the thrift shop I buy several narrow belts, at ten cents each, in leather, stretch fabric, and plastic. I invent various ID devices; I tape to one of the belts a label with my name printed on it, Maxie's name, our phone number, and the plea: "Please return!" I use an ice pick to punch holes in the belt, I adjust the length for comfort, for security, for safety.

Maxie sits patiently while I make him try on one and another of these potential collars while I jiggle my finger under it (nearly choking him) to make sure it's not too loose, not too tight. Then, for double safety, I make him another collar out of pink elastic, just in case he slips out of one. On this one I write my phone number in indelible ballpoint ink. I can't be too careful.

I then have second thoughts. Should Maxie be dressed in thrift shop outfits? If *I* want to dress that way, it's my business, but should I foist these values on him, force second-hand apparel on this sleek, beautiful, shapely, first-rate, first-class purebred Manx kitten? Maxie is *class*, Maxie should have the attire commensurate with his status.

~

When I'm out shopping, I stop at the Pet Emporium and see the ranks of collars displayed like jewelry. They come in chartreuse, shocking pink, blood red, sky blue, sea green, and serious, solemn black. They come in many styles; the nylon ones have an insert of black elastic, which is designed for that desperate moment when the cat gets his collar stuck on a tree branch and can't extricate himself. The insert will snap open and set him free. (In the same way, the insert may allow him to lose his collar and run about in the world unidentified!)

I am amazed again at this universe of designer litter boxes, designer toys, designer raincoats, designer cat abodes. For those who wish to offer their cat first-class sleeping accommodations, there are four-story cat-apartments, with Pullman berths, rocket-shaped rooms, upholstered cushions.

Poor Maxie: he can have an old pillow in a laundry basket if he desires, he can play with a killer-shoulder-pad toy. He's part of our family, and since we don't shop for ourselves where the jet-set go, he'll have to be satisfied being supported in the style to which we are accustomed!

March 15

Today is my birthday. Two girlfriends take me to lunch; we talk about how old we seem to be getting without our permission, how annoyed we are at the system, and how we can't believe we're not all still seventeen. We decide that in our old age we will jointly buy one of those old motels in the country that they used to call "motor courts" and each of us will live in our own little cabin and we'll cook wonderful meals together.

My fortune cookie says: "Today is your lucky day." We laugh and toast one another with green tea. I invite them to come to the nursing home with me, but my friends decline.

~

The moment my mother sees me she says: "Happy birthday, I wish you had a better mother than me."

"How could I have a better mother than I already have?"

"A mother who could have gotten out of bed and called you this morning to wish you happy birthday."

I tell her I'm happy she's my mother, happy I was born, happy I have had all the birthdays I've been blessed to have, including this one.

"What do you want for a present?"

"I have myself," I say. "See the pink bow on top of my head? I'm my own present. You gave me me."

I open my canvas carry-case and extract one of the chocolate-iced cupcakes I baked last night. "Here's the birthday cake I made for myself," I tell her. "This cupcake is especially for you."

"I can't eat it," she says. "I don't eat, you know."

"Then smell the chocolate icing." I let the cupcake graze her nose and she smells.

"Take it home," she says. "I can't eat it."

I toss the cupcake into the waste basket. Sometimes I think I ought to give up trying to please her. Just stop.

∾

J. and I are going out for the evening, to the screening of a TV movie written by a friend of ours. At first I lock Maxie in the laundry room, with his toy parrot (the one wearing the grass skirt), with his striped/stuffed snake, with a bowl of food, but he protests so vigorously, meows so heartrendingly, that I decide to take a chance, to give him the run of the whole house.

He dashes into the living room and immediately curls up on one of the rugs, eyeing us, waiting for whatever insult we intend to cause him. He knows, or seems to know, we're leaving.

J. is nervous about giving him such freedom. He knows we could find the house hanging in shreds by the time we get back. But he seems willing to let me decide; maybe he trusts Maxie to exercise his best judgment.

∾

As I watch the movie, I find I can't concentrate. I find myself missing Maxie. Viscerally. I think of how he lays his paw upon my neck, or reaches up with it to pat my chin. I think of how he peers into my face with his expressive eyes, watching for what? (What does he see? Is he reading my soul, or wondering if that nose upon my face is a toy, to be jumped for and bitten?) But I want him in my arms. I want to stroke his silken fur. Is this love? Have I fallen in love? Am I becoming a daffy, besmitten cat lover, worse than any adoring grandmother? It's true that I pull out photos of him wherever I go.

On the way home I can almost taste the pleasure of our reunion. I'll find him in some corner of the house. I'll cry, "Hello, Maxie! How I've missed you." J. will look at me and wonder how I became such a mushy marshmallow.

March 18

When Maxie fell asleep on my chest last night, his rump, at first, was in my face, which made me laugh. Later he turned around so that his face was nestled in the curve of my chin. Each time I took a breath, the hairs of his ear would stir and he'd twitch his ear fiercely. Yet he did not change position. I'd breathe, he'd twitch, but still he'd stay unmoving, his eyes closed. Something about his determination to continue sleeping (and his trust in me) impressed me.

I am impressed by Maxie. Being so close to him then, my eyes unable to focus, his face hugely filling the horizon of my vision, he seemed to me as big as the earth itself, as majestic as a sphinx, larger than life. I whispered to him, "Are you a god?" The upward curve of his mouth, a fraction of an inch from my eyes, seemed knowing. "Were you sent here to lead my mother to the other side?"

My inquiry did not seem insane to me, nor did talking to him this way, softly, in the dream state of my breathing and his breathing. His head filled the sky above me, his striped mysterious face was intense with wisdom and grace. Why not Maxie as God?

Maxie does not know fear in the abstract; only fear as it presents itself in the form of a noise, a movement, a shadow. He does not fear the future, or loss, or his death, or my death—he lives totally in the moment, in the pure essence of it, having only that experience and no other. "Be Here Now" is the name of my friend Stephanie's cat. Maxie is here now.

~

My mother, today, is crying out as I come up the hall: "Nurse! Nurse!"

"What do you need, Mom?"

"When is the doctor coming to take out the staples?"

"I don't know. He'll come when he comes. They never say in advance when they'll come to the nursing home. They fit it into their days."

"This is no way to live," she says. "I can't move. I can't blow my nose. I can't wash my hands."

"I know, Mom."

"One of the nurses said to me, 'Never have surgery again. You've been through too much already.'"

"You have been through a lot, Mom. That's true."

"She said I would have to sign a form to give permission for surgery, and I should never do it again. She said I've had enough to last me all my life."

"I think you have, too."

Her white hair is brushed back over her forehead. She looks peaceful. She says, "I hate the shower. They have to get me first into a wheelchair, then into the shower chair. The water is too hot, then it's too cold. They don't feel it like we do."

"They" is Elena, the Mexican aide who showers her. We have gone over this before.

"They feel everything, Mom. They're just like we are. But maybe your skin is more sensitive than hers."

"In the night," she says, "I sometimes want to ring the buzzer just so someone will come in and talk to me. But there's no one to talk to here. No one."

"Maybe we should get you a phone." (I say it but don't mean it. My sister and I have talked about this.)

"No, because who would I have to call? My children. I'd bother you all the time. You'd hear the phone ring and you'd say, 'Oh no, that's my mother again.'"

"My, you are a sharp cookie, Mom. You anticipate all the moves. You even read minds."

"Yes," she says with satisfaction. "Because I know how things are."

March 19

We are going away for three days to visit our daughter, Susanna, in Berkeley. Maxie must be left behind, but what shall we do with him? To board him in a kennel is impossible; to imagine him locked in a small cage for three days, yowling with loneliness, is intolerable.

In the past we often went away and left our two veteran cats, Korky and Big Kitty, outside, in confidence that they would be well fed by a hired neighbor-child, would entertain themselves in the great outdoors, and would find easy shelter if it should rain. (Our neighbor has a large garden shed, a covered potting area, and cozy shelves for the cats to sleep upon.)

But Maxie—only five months old or thereabouts—is too tiny to be left alone outside for three days, too delicate emotionally (in my opinion) to be left alone in the laundry room with only the brooms for company. I tell J. my concerns and he reminds me that we can't stay home forever just because we have a new kitten.

Why not? I think.

~

I impose upon my sister, who lives nearby, to be Maxie's surrogate mother. Not only must he be fed, he must be talked to, cooed over, petted, played with, adored.

"Of course," she says. "Adored for sure. Anything else?"

"And make sure you dangle his stuffed parrot—the one with the grass skirt—for him."

"Without a doubt," she says.

"And wiggle his stuffed snake, so he thinks it's alive."

"I would never do less."

"And you might even read to him. He likes *The Owl and the Pussycat.*"

"Would you like me to sign a contract before you leave?"

"That's okay," I tell her. "I trust you."

❧

During the night I hear coyotes crying in the distant hills. One bone-chilling cry blends with another in a terrible chorus of threat. I've been told they come down from the hills for water and food . . . and when necessary for little kittens. I hold my breath and listen: they seem to be coming closer. I wonder if Maxie, curled on his cushion in the laundry room, is afraid. I can imagine him holding his head up, his ears pointed, his little heart pounding, shaking the delicate harp of his rib cage.

I tell myself all living creatures have to deal with night-fears. I myself have many. He will have to learn to cope. Maybe there is a cat-mantra that will calm him. Maybe he counts sheep, or little mice. Maybe he imagines butterflies in a meadow when he is afraid. Who can tell?

❧

By morning, I have decided not to leave him confined in the laundry room, but instead will give him the run of the entire house. He's completely trained in using his litter box, so that's not a concern. If I leave him free in the house, I will be reassured that at least he'll have more venues to entertain him. He'll be able to see out of every window, and thus be mentally stimulated and physically secure. I don't actually discuss this decision with J., but I let him see my preparations. (Perhaps I hope he will not pay attention.) But, after all, we left Maxie free in the house just a few days ago without dire results. Why not now?

～

Before we actually leave, I turn the radio in the kitchen to the classical music station and adjust the volume to a soothing level. I sprinkle a little catnip on Maxie's scratching post. I cover all the furniture with blankets, sheets and old coats. At zero hour, my heart is in my mouth as I lift him up, hug him, kiss the little pink heart of his nose, tell him I love him. *Oh, Maxie, I promise I will come back to you. Goodbye, Beloved. Parting is such sweet sorrow.*

～

When we return late on the third day, we find Maxie sleeping happily on the couch. He has not had a nervous breakdown. He has not turned into a wild, hostile animal. He stretches and yawns, he greets me without resentment or anger, he does not shun me. In fact, he hardly notices me. He unearths a daddy-longlegs in the corner and gets busy harassing it. When it flees, he discovers an ant, then an invisible speck takes his attention. I can see that he's kept himself entertained for days. He has torn the grass skirt of his stuffed parrot to shreds, but the furniture is intact. The empty cat-food cans in the garbage bag attest to my sister's kindness and Maxie's good appetite. I have an inkling that my sister has played with him and loved him more than a little!

I know I should give him time to get used to our return, but I can't contain myself. I grab him up, gobble him down, coo, and kiss him. "Are you my baby?" I croon. "Are you my little itty bitty darling? Did you miss me? Did you miss your mommy? Are you my cookie-wookie?"

He takes it well, considering. He allows my excess, and even licks my cheek once or twice, waiting it out. Then—after a decent interval—he leaps out of my arms and runs to the back door.

"Out! Out!" he begs by twitching his little stumpy tail. So I let him out into the sunshine of the yard, and watch him scramble up the yew tree. When he reaches the top, he sticks his tiny striped face out between the branches and mews at me. J. is watching, smiling. The sun is shining and all's right with the world.

March 27

After dark Maxie is possessed by the devil. Something comes over him, a spell, a veil of enchantment—something so powerful that he can't be still, but runs through the house, from one end to the other, making a sound at the door not like a cat, but almost like a crow—a cawing sound, from deep in his throat, low and intense. A kind of wild need is in it, even pain, something primitive and desperate.

I let him out tonight, not intentionally, but because I open the door to feed Big Kitty and Maxie darts through the opening. He is so fast! Now you see him, now you don't. I rush out after him, but already he's in front of me, he's behind me, he's here, he's there, he's gone. It seems I have blind spots everywhere in my vision because I can't seem to follow his movements. I see him and I lose him as he dashes in a frenzy from a tree to a bush to the ivy to the side of the house.

"Maxie! Maxie! Come here!"

He looks at me without recognition, his eyes wide, hostile, full of doubt. "It's me, Maxie. Look, remember me?"

Clearly he doesn't.

I come inside and get a flashlight. I get a bowl of meat scraps, I go out and hunt, I call, I beg, I cajole. Maxie is like a bat, darting, disappearing, reappearing, his pointed little ears hearing alarms I can't decipher.

I am getting tired, irritated. It's night, you dummy, I think. Coyotes are on the loose. It's going to rain tonight. Let's stop this nonsense.

A passing car's motor seems to terrify him, the flash of the head-lights is a menace that freezes him in his tracks. I take a hint from this and paralyze him in the beam of my flashlight. At the same time I shout fiercely: "Maxie, don't you dare move!" He doesn't. He stares transfixed till I lift him in one hand and encircle him with the other. "In the house we go! Right now. Don't wiggle, I mean business, Buddy."

~

Inside the house, I make it up to him. A program comes on public television, "Nature: Cats" is the name of it. Maxie and I watch it from my bed, his little solid form cuddled on my chest. He seems to be falling asleep till he hears sounds of meows, of wild creatures, and then he turns around to watch the TV himself, head held high, eyes focused on the screen, his little tail just in front of my eyes.

A Manx female is shown in excited sexual receptiveness; she raises her tail to the male, he steps above her, takes her ruff in his mouth, steadies her by the pressure of his forelegs, and mates with her. She cries out, she bats him away, she screams her pleasure and anger. Maxie stands up—alert—on the bed. From the light in his eyes, I see that he has heard the call of the wild. I realize that he's old enough to be altered. I'd better arrange for it.

March 28

Tonight J. comes with me to the nursing home. My mother smiles only once during our visit, and that's after I show her the pictures of Maxie: Maxie yawning, Maxie in my lap on his back (all four legs held limply in the air), Maxie on the patio steps, his head down, his forepaws crossed in the delicate pose of a ballet dancer. My mother says to me, "He really makes you happy, doesn't he?"

I admit he does, which is when she smiles. What mother doesn't want to hear that her child has been made happy? I feel I have given her something useful when all the useful things I have brought her have been rejected. The radio sits untouched on the little dresser beside her bed. ("Take it away," she always tells me, "or someone will steal it.") After giving all the arguments I could think of *("You might want to listen to it, I might want to listen to it, you could find some pretty piano music to listen to, you could hear the news")* and she had given me all *her* arguments *("I don't want to listen to music anymore, piano music breaks my heart now that I can't play, the news is all murders and shootings and rapes, why should I listen to it?"),* I finally agreed to take the radio home, only to find it had been chained to the dresser and fastened by a security screw.

I had shopped the thrift shops for weeks to find that radio—it needed to have the lightest-touch on/off button so that my mother, without any strength in her fingers, could manage to turn it off and on. And I'd bought it for five dollars, telling her it had only cost one—so that if it were stolen it would be no loss at all.

Lying to my mother. A bad thing to do, of course. How much lying is lying, how much omission of truth is lying? How much ignoring of the truth is lying? What does a woman of my age owe—in the way of truth—to her 85-year-old mother?

My mother is not happy with one picture in the group of pictures I'm showing her—the one an aide took of me with my mother on my birthday this month. I had leaned down over the bed so that our foreheads were touching, my earrings tilting at a strange angle, my features slightly lopsided.

"The less I see of myself, the better I like it," she says. "When I see my face, it frightens me." J. is having a hard time finding anything to say. He sits silently in the orange plastic chair. We are planning to go out to dinner afterward, and I tell my mother this.

"I eat nothing anymore. Not even chocolate ice cream."

I consider her existence once again (as if I ever stop). She does not eat, does not walk, cannot move her right hand, no longer writes, can't play her beloved music, cannot make a phone call, does not go to the bathroom, is unable to wash her own face, open a window to feel the breeze, cannot, cannot, cannot. . . .

"My life is like an open village," she says. "Anyone can put their hands on me. These things that are very private to me, eating, going to the bathroom, they take care of it, whether I want it or not. I don't know what to do. I can't take poison, I have no poison here."

"Would you take poison if you had it?"

"I can't take anything by mouth," she replies, neatly avoiding the issue. "Besides, I don't have a poison pill."

Well, *I* don't have a poison pill, either, so I feel absolved of any complicity in the matter. But what if she asked me, someday, to get her one?

I begin talking about dinner; I tell my mother about our two-for-one coupon book, I explain and explain and explain. This performance I'm called upon to give is why my visits to her exhaust me. From the moment I walk into her room, I am on stage. I have to tap dance and sing, have to project my voice, clarify the scene I am describing, make it fast and peppy and interesting and entertaining.

She watches my eyes, searching my face for . . . what? Is she surprised at how old I am? At how foreign I seem to her? How familiar? What does she think of me? Does she think of me at all, or only of herself, her plight?

"I love you," I say as we leave her room.

"I love you both," she says. The other ancient woman in the room lies silent in her bed, and we wave to her. She is staring at the lilies someone brought her. Easter is coming. The world's calendar proceeds, Christmas is past, Easter is arriving, the world turns.

∼

J. and I go to a Mexican restaurant and order fajitas, shrimp, and sirloin steak, expensive items, and they come sizzling on a black cast-iron skillet, fragrant with onions and red peppers and the scent of grilled meat. We order Mexican beer, we toast one another.

"To our health."

"To our happy life together."

And all too aware of what comes at the end of life, we eat hungrily, with great appetite, smiling at one another, offering our forks to share bites of this and that, relishing, enjoying, delighting in this most ordinary of pleasures, our food, and each other's company.

April 1

I seem to resist recognizing that Maxie's childhood is over. Or at least his kittenhood. For the last few days he has scorned all his toys: his killer shoulder-pad, his parrot with the shredded grass skirt, his fuzzy troll, his pennies in a film container, his stuffed snake. When in the house he paces nervously, from window to door to window to door. Something is changing.

～

Tonight, when I go out with the garbage after dinner, Maxie darts out the front door and scurries for cover in the dense bushes at the end of the front yard. The night continues to sing him its siren song. I call his name and he peers at me as if he'd never seen me before. His eyes are round, full of suspicion and distrust of a high order.

The headlights of a car wash over the grass and Maxie freezes; his eyes glow green, so intense they almost seem red. He makes a run for it. I hear the scratching sound of his claws on bark; he's climbing one of the trees. Is it the pecan tree? The orange tree? I catch sight of him on a high limb of the rubber tree.

"Maxie!" I cry. "What is this?" I reach toward him, but he moves higher.

Okay, never mind, I think. I'll go in and then you'll come down.

Much later, two hours later, I see him looking in his food dish at the back door. I pretend we never had this falling out. I open the door slowly and say, "Hi, Maxie, want to come in?"

He trots right in. I close the door. I swoop him up in my arms. "The prodigal son has returned," I say to him. He twists out of my arms and jumps down. He goes to the door as if he had not just had this sudden, high-tension adventure, as if he would like to be let out anew, and be allowed to begin all over again.

~

In the morning, J. and I both notice a terrible smell in the family room. Big Kitty has been roaming in there and so has Maxie. But Big Kitty was altered twelve years ago—can he possibly have sprayed? Or is it Maxie, now seven months old, who has sprayed? In any case, the smell is bad enough that I think we will have to chop off this room of the house in order to get rid of it.

After J. leaves for work, I try to find the source of the smell. I get down on my hands and knees and put my nose to the rug. I creep around, sniffing the edges of the couch, the chairs, the coffee table, the TV. The smell is generalized but stronger than ever; I can't describe it, it's like nothing I have ever smelled before. It's incredibly potent. It means business.

But how can I wash it away if I can't find it? I see nothing (the rug is brown), and one moment it seems to be coming from one place, the next from another.

I dig out of some cabinet my ancient rusty can of room deodorizer, and I begin spraying at the walls, hitting the spider webs on the ceiling, shooting under the couch, spinning myself in a circle. I hold my breath as droplets of the vile stuff come floating down upon me. This fake perfume smells worse in some ways than the original foul smell. But I'm determined to override the stench. I close up the room and run to the other end of the house to breathe.

~

By the time J. comes home, there are two awful smells in the room.

"Don't worry," I tell him. "I'll air it out."

I push open the two sliding doors on either side of the room and let the sunshine come in. And the wind. And the scent of spring flowers. This can't last forever. We definitely know who has been remiss. I should have had Maxie altered before this, but I was afraid to face up to it.

Now I study Maxie's little nervous face and I call the animal hospital. I make an appointment for next week. All right. He will face the razor's cut. It's time. Never mind that his little Manx genes will be lost to history; never mind that he'll never know the pleasures of roaming in the night to find his true love, that he won't yowl the cat cries of passion that we sometimes hear in the wee hours.

General wisdom has it that an altered cat is a better pet. He won't roam, won't fight, won't disappear for days at a time . . . and won't spray in the house. General wisdom is also self-serving; if we fix him, it's better for us.

April 5

In heavy morning traffic, Maxie and I drive to the place where he will be de-manned, emasculated, castrated (or in the gentle terms of the industry: altered). To what will he be altered, and from what? When I come to claim him ("not before five" as the instructions say, ". . . and we consider it advisable to keep him overnight, if possible") will he have emerged from the netherworld of anaesthesia as a werewolf? A wild cheetah? A pumpkin, perhaps?

"He won't feel a thing," the receptionist assures me, peering into the carrier as if to be sure I'm not trying to fool her, haven't left it empty, or put in a raccoon or a possum. "It won't bother him at all."

"They said the same thing when I had my hysterectomy," I think I should tell her. "But did they ever call me later to ask?"

~

Reverberating in my ears is the sound Maxie made as I stuffed him, hindquarters first, into the plastic Pet Taxi in preparation to taking him to his "fixing." (Another odd term: nothing whatsoever is broken in this healthy, energetic kitten.) He hung by his claws to prevent my getting him in, and when I closed the door on him, he let out a howl that proved he was sorry he had ever allowed me to clip his claws, count his baby teeth, or have any access whatsoever to his body.

Even so, when I lifted the Pet Taxi by its handle, Maxie scuffled inside and slid to one end like an unbalanced load in a tram car. At that moment, I knew his love for me was not unconditional.

~

As a way of sympathizing with Maxie's ordeal, I spend the morning taking a medical test I have long needed to attend to. An echocardiogram has been scheduled for me for months, and I choose this day to get it out of the way. As electrodes are pasted on my chest, I think about how the miracles of modern medicine take us into regions our ancestors never knew. A clear gel is smeared on my left breast as well as on the rolling wand the technician holds. In ancient times, Maxie would have got to keep his testicles and I would have been spared seeing my mitral valve flap on the screen like an animated flipper. From time to time the efficient woman at the side of the bed on which I recline presses a button on her console and I hear, not only see, my heart beating: *whoosh tick tick, whoosh tick tick.*

Knowing better, I ask, "Can you tell me what you see?" and of course she says, "Only the doctor can tell you what the test shows."

"Isn't it a pity?" I ask her.

~

After I am dressed again, I try to find my way to the nursing home on unfamiliar streets, but take a wrong turn and end up driving through a county park. A man walking a dog on the edge of a dry pond calls out and the dog bounds toward him. The dog is male; I wonder if they "fix" dogs as often as they do cats. All my cat books assure me that I am doing Maxie a favor—saving him from nights of wandering for miles after strange females, saving him from savage fights with other horny tomcats, saving him from aggressive tendencies that a radical reduction in testosterone will spare him. But it can't be denied that I also will spare him from the pleasures of mating with a female of his species and from the privilege that living creatures are born with of being able to procreate their own kind. This is the heaviness in my heart.

~

My mother is agitated that they left her in her wheelchair too long. She has a litany of abuses to report, all of which I am sure are true, but can't be changed or prevented. I try to distract her by offering her some chocolate mints, by trying to get some music on the radio I bought her, which is still affixed by a chain to her little table. She says the chocolate mint tastes bitter and asks to spit it out. She says she doesn't like the music that's on—the only kind of music she likes is piano music, and this is orchestral music. I turn off the radio. I show her a photocopy of a picture of my youngest daughter, and offer to leave it on her wall; no, someone will steal it. I assure her it's only a copy of a picture; I can make another copy if it's stolen. No, is the answer. I want nothing here, nothing pleasant, nothing that reminds me of my old life, nothing from the world outside, nothing, nothing, because my life is nothing.

I haven't the energy to argue, though sometimes I do. Her life *is* nothing; how can I contest that? *I* am—perhaps—her life, and obviously it's not enough. I tell her I have to pick up Maxie, now irrevocably changed, fixed, and altered.

"I think he'll be in pain," she says. "I know what that's like."

~

When I arrive to take my kitten home from the vet's, he's not quite ready. I wait, looking through the scrapbook on the counter of the animal hospital, a book filled with joyous pictures of groomed and beribboned pets whom the vet (or the corporation of vets) has, ostensibly, saved from tragic illnesses. They are all so healthy and grateful-looking. Then Maxie is brought out to me, limp as a melting candle, bleary-eyed, bedraggled, and the doctor's helper stuffs him into the carry-case like a bundle of rags. She hands me a checklist of possible dangers to be watched for: nausea and vomiting, blood in the urine, infection, swelling at the site of the incision. I am to call at once if he is not eating, is lethargic, or if he cries in pain.

He is crying in pain, right now, in fact.

"I thought there was nothing to it," I remark to the helper, who is wearing an apron decorated with little smiling kittens. "I thought they don't feel a thing."

"Oh, they don't," she insists. "Cats have a very high pain threshold." (This reminds me of how fishermen swear that a fish doesn't feel the hook in the membrane of its mouth.) She proceeds to assure me that cats live in the "now" and don't even remember what occurred ten minutes ago. But though my Maxie may be living in the now *now*, he is eyeing me as he tries to hold his eyes open, with a bitter question. How did this come to pass? How did he come from a happy cat who a few hours ago was frolicking among the butterflies in the back yard, to this limp and exhausted creature collapsed in the Pet Taxi?

∾

At home I deposit him not on his cushion in the laundry basket on top of the clothes dryer (I can see that for him, in his present state, this is far too high a perch) but on the fluffy bath mat in the bathroom. He's both bloodied and bowed; he defers to my choices, he puts his nose down, makes a sorrowful moan, and closes his eyes.

∾

He takes it hard, my Maxie. He doesn't bounce back in a few hours; it takes him five days to regain his appetite, the sparkle in his eyes, the mischief in his twitching ears. We've paid our price and done the right thing for mankind (and for catkind), but we both want it known that Maxie will not be passing on his special, precious genes to the next generation, he didn't "not feel a thing," and he is indeed "altered" in a way that stays in his memory. When he happens to glimpse the "Pet Taxi" in the broom closet, he hisses as if it is no less a threat to him than a rattlesnake. I take it out to the garage and hide it there. It's the least I can do for him.

April 14

Springtime has arrived with a trumpet call! The garden has burst forth with color and fragrance; the plum tree whose old branches are brittle and dry has magically sprouted new growth from its black tips, and tiny green teardrop-shaped baby plums are arching into the sunshine. The wisteria vine (nowhere near as vast as the world-famous vine that resides in this city and is listed in a book of world records) decorates the fence and intertwines with the branches of the tall eucalyptus tree. The nectarine tree (whose branches I have leashed together with various outgrown belts of my children) is lopsided but fruitful. Still, somewhere in the mystery of its growth each summer, scars and veins appear on each fruit, and by the time they are ripe, they are worm-drilled and bird-pecked.

In the far end of the yard there's also a lush apricot tree which never bears fruit. Years ago a friend told me to feed it copper; my children tossed pennies at its base, which still—to this day—lie in the soil.

The yard holds much of our family history—the swing set, sunken irretrievably in cement, the grave of Korky, the golden tabby who found us, like all the others, by Pure Fate. His grave is kept company by numerous unmarked graves as well, of pet birds, mice, frogs, even goldfish. My youngest daughter grieved at every passing, rejoiced at the arrival of each new pet, never refusing to repeat the cycle, always willing to go through each love affair, and each parting.

Big Kitty finds it just another springtime; he's getting too old to rejoice, preferring now to lie sleepily in the sun, confident of the length of the season and of his place in it.

But Maxie! He is wild! He is healed and well now from his surgical setback, and each morning leaps from his bed on the dryer and makes a beeline to the sliding door to the yard. No more does he nuzzle my chin as I come to greet him where he rises from his pillow, no more does he pause to lick my cheek with his sandpaper tongue; he does not even pause to check his food dish, but makes a mad dash right to the glass door, every hair on his back alert, waiting for me to unlock and open it for him.

I have brought him the equivalent of an Easter bonnet, a new rainbow-colored collar and his own personalized printed dog tag (cat tag?) that says, in big letters, MAXIE, on a little plastic smiling cat-face. (Beneath it is my name and phone number.) Maxie doesn't know how pretty he looks in that bright new collar, but he knows he doesn't like the tag, which swings just out of reach below his chin and makes a clackety sound whenever he lowers his head to the food dish.

He looks big now. His hind legs have grown long and powerful, his cheeks have rounded out, his markings seem brighter. His chin is clearly white now, and the angular raccoon-mask stripes beside his eyes are black and brilliant. Concentric circles travel down his chest like rows of royal jewels. When he sits straight-backed like a statue, front legs close together, it seems as if he has been cut out of a single swatch of woven cloth; the black stripes of his forelegs match perfectly, he is a model of symmetry and beauty.

~

But is Maxie's kittenhood truly over? I don't want to believe that it's time to put away his toys. He now ignores his scratching post in favor of the exquisite rough bark of the pepper tree, the inviting roughness of the palm tree, the thin upper twigs of the orange and the plum trees. He shuns the killer shoulder-pad in favor of a grasshopper on the patio, turns his nose up at the film container with pennies inside—preferring the click of a cricket in the ivy.

His famous stuffed parrot, even when liberally sprinkled with catnip, cannot hold a candle to the blue jay squawking in the tree as it sees Maxie's spiky tail twitching, as it watches Maxie standing in the grass planning his strategy for a strike.

How quickly my baby became a man! How fast he turned into an adolescent, all strut and bravado, all cocky independence, all energy and daring and wanting to stay out late! Because now it's the rule: whenever I call him in at night, he bolts away, in the opposite direction. Wherever I am, he wants to go the other way! Whatever I say he pretends not to hear. Whatever I offer (tuna, sardines, hot dogs) he rejects. He has better things to do. *Go inside,* he tells me by the dismissive flip of his jaunty tail. *I am a creature of the night. My destiny calls.*

April 16

My mother is in a good mood when I visit in the evening. She has been watching *Jeopardy* and *Wheel of Fortune* and says she has already won a trip to Greece and a trip to France. She tells me an "ombudsman" has visited her and encouraged her to draw up a Power of Attorney for Health Care. I tell her she already has one, and that if she can't make health decisions for herself, I will make them for her. She already wears on her wrist a red plastic bracelet, proclaiming "Do Not Resuscitate."

There's a new roommate in the room. The last one has died. In fact, Sunday night when I visited my mother and glanced at the roommate, I thought to myself, *She looks dead.* I had stood beside the woman's bed, where the clothes closets are, hanging up my mother's laundered robes. The woman's mouth was open, her cheeks sunken, her skin pasty. This is not the first time my mother has been in a room when death visited. But she's unconcerned; what it means to her is that the loud TV won't be played any longer.

But I have an image of Death, Himself, in the room, waiting to descend and carry the old woman away. He could just as well have selected my mother as the other old woman, whose first name, it so happens, was the same as mine.

∾

The new roommate, named Naomi, has suffered a stroke, but she's feisty, raunchy; this is perhaps what has animated my mother. They've been talking! I realize it's been months since my mother has had anyone to talk to but me or my sister.

Naomi says to me, "My first husband, he only knew me fifteen minutes when he proposed marriage to me."

"He must have loved you at first sight."

"He loved my boobs," Naomi says. "I had quite a pair. Of course they're down to my knees now."

My mother is looking over at her in shock. I laugh. I hope this new roommate will be good for her. This lady has a love of life that perhaps can rub off on my mother, even at this late date.

April 19

Tonight we have our first springtime barbecue on the patio. There's something festive about eating outside in the light of dusk, the coals glowing in the cast iron stove, the new moon gleaming in the sky. While J. puts ribs and chicken on the grate, Maxie prowls in the bushes at the outskirts of the yard, rushing back to check on the activities and then to disappear into the brush.

Company arrives, my sister, my nephew, my daughter and her husband. There is the constant opening and closing of the sliding screen door as we carry out the pickles and olives, the dill potatoes and the spinach salad, the coleslaw and the sliced tomatoes, the paper plates and the plastic glasses and the bucket of ice cubes and the cans of soft drinks.

So much work, just to eat out under the sky. Yet we do it happily to see the darkness creep upon the world, to feel the first feathery stings of the mosquitoes, to know the ants are waiting in their sandy hills to find the scraps of food after we have gone in.

Maxie plays hide and seek with us, darting between our legs, daring us to catch him, dashing out into the darkness. By this time of night I always have him inside (if all goes according to plan), but tonight he senses permission and takes advantage of it.

I think this is good for him, to know we are close by, but to have the freedom to be a night-hunter. No coyote would dare to come by while we are all sitting around, eating and laughing.

We are jolly and good-natured, all of us; we're starving, but for some reason the ribs aren't cooking—they seem to stay a bloody red. The coals are weaklings, they aren't burning hot, the grate is too high and it's too late to take everything off and put it in its lowered position, so we're just going to have to wait. (At least I precooked the chicken earlier in the microwave, in order not to find it charred and crisp outside, pink and watery at the bone.) J. hovers over the ribs, turning them this way and that as if he is imploring them to do the right thing—get cooked.

But we don't mind waiting; we savor the fresh air, we feel the wind stirring the wind chimes (four hanging pewter cats and one hanging fish. Shouldn't the odd chime be a bird? Why a fish, hanging in midair?).

Big Kitty comes by, swishing his fluffy tail, asking for what he always asks for, food, food, food, but there is nothing to give him yet. Maxie, on the other hand, takes food for granted; the first thing he wants from me in the morning is attention, a hug, a kiss. He wants to nibble my chin from his perch in the basket on the dryer, he wants to climb up on my chest, inch by inch, till his front paws are on my shoulders and he is high enough to nuzzle my nose. When I blink at him, he makes a tiny "meow" of acknowledgment. He seems to expect and trust that food will be forthcoming, in large amounts, and without question. Big Kitty has the attitude that he can never have enough, that I will never *give* him enough, that in his world even enough is never enough.

I appreciate Maxie's casual attitude toward food; I share his belief that there's much more of interest to explore in the world.

The whole night lies before him: moths and night birds, owls and peacocks. In fact, we hear the cries of the peacocks now, a high whining chorus of them, sounding almost like cats' meows. A great population of wild peacocks has exploded in our city: they have bred lustily in the county arboretum and now roam the streets and side-walks, taking their time, stopping the traffic. On our walk last week J. and I saw a group of them in someone's front yard, six dun-colored females and two males, one young, with a sparse tail feather fan to offer, and the other magnificent, enormous, bursting with ego. We stopped to watch as he unfolded his fan of feathers, shimmered them with an enticing rattle and jangle, like the clicking of tiny metallic castanets. He posed, he paused, he turned slowly in a circle like a fashion model, alert to whom he might impress, waiting for one of the females to succumb to him, or at least to show respect. Instead, they all walked away to peck in the dirt! He followed, rather awkwardly, with all those accessories to squeeze between the bushes in the yard, and he stopped again to rattle his finery, but they would have none of it.

Now Maxie cocks his ears to their cries. What could that be, he seems to be asking, is it threat or prey? He listens, he waits, and then he decides it's too far away to worry about, or that they're not coming his way. (I find myself thinking I know what he's thinking, but it's only my human thought overlaid on his feline behavior.)

Finally the ribs get that black edge to them. The fat drips and flares on the coals, the aroma of barbecue sauce incinerating floats temptingly in the air.

"They're ready!" J. declares triumphantly, waving one of them on a long-handled fork, and the rib flies into the air like a missile and lands almost on Maxie's head. He takes off like an arrow shot from a bow. He's out of here! He's gone! A hot bone has dive-bombed on him from out of nowhere. And to think he was worried a moment ago about the cry of a peacock.

We all laugh, as Big Kitty sniffs the hot rib, waits patiently till he can handle it, and then drags it off the patio onto the grass, where he begins to tear away at it. He's too sophisticated in the ways of the world to think it was a comet falling; he knows how J. cooks! He has attended many of our barbecues, and seen many hot dogs fly off into space.

Long after the guests have gone and I've collected the paper plates in trash bags and packed away the leftover food, long after the coals have been reduced to white ash, just as I am about to fall exhausted into bed, I remember that Maxie is out! What a mother I am, to have forgotten her child! To have assumed or imagined that he was somewhere in the house (which he usually is at this late hour), or not to have assumed anything, to have simply not thought of him! I am appalled, and I run to get my flashlight and go out and look for him.

While I am prowling the large back yard, I wish I had done what I once thought would be a good idea, attached a little bell to his collar so that, like a roaming cow with a cowbell, he could be located when I needed to find him. Big Kitty is already sleeping deeply on the lounge chair; for some reason, probably because he has been an outside cat for so many years, I feel no worry about his survival, imagine that no coyote would ever tangle with him and expect to get away with its eyes intact. But Maxie is another matter—he weighs five and a half pounds, he can only scramble halfway up a thick tree before he has a change of heart or loses his balance.

The yard is vast and silent. He is not here. I go back through the house and open the front door, and Maxie's eyes glow iridescent-green in the beam of my flashlight.

"So there you are!" I cry, already weak with relief, feeling as if I have already swooped him up in my arms and hugged him against my chest. But as I move toward him, he disappears. He's like an image on a screen, clicked on, and then off. Where is he? "Maxie!" I cry. "Come in. Come here." I see a flash, and he's at the border of the ivy of the front yard, another flash, and he's under the mock orange tree, another flash and he's gone entirely.

I see this will be a battle of wills. It has happened before. We are at a stand-off; he has the advantage. I'm just a big, awkward human being with a flashlight, and he's a dart of energy, willfully disregarding what I want, which is to take him in and put him in a small room, in a small basket, on a small pillow. I tend to see his point, irritated as I am. Why would anyone want to give up this enormous bed of night for that?

"Maxie," I say, "there are big, bad animals outside at night. Raccoons eat the cat food you leave over, possums come to find the crumbs they leave behind. There are owls in the trees waiting to lift you up in their talons." (Is this true? Wouldn't Maxie be too big for an owl? I will have to consult my nature books.)

Now I see him! He's hunched under a bush in a place I can't reach. I try my wiles, I say, "Food, Maxie," in the tone I use to call him to his dinner, but yes—we know by now that food is not his main temptation. What does he care? Besides, I have no food with me and he may know it.

I go inside and J. sees me opening a can of sardines.

"Still hungry after that big dinner?" he asks me.

"Very funny. I'm trying to catch Maxie. Can you help?"

Now there are two of us in the front yard, armed with flashlights, sardines, little stuffed toys of his. We take positions at opposite ends of the property—one of us will flush him out and the other will catch him. There are the two of us, cajoling, begging, enticing him one minute, calling out sternly and fiercely the next. Maxie is involved with a night crawler, some little beetle-like bug he's batting around in the dirt.

J. has only limited patience with this; he wants to go in and watch the eleven o'clock news. I have more endurance, but even mine is running out.

Finally, we give up. We leave the two dishes of sardines on the front step and go inside. *Okay, this is good-bye, Maxie.* I make my private good-byes, I imagine the funeral (we'll bury him next to Korky), I imagine I will have to buy a black dress since I don't have one, I wonder what music we will play at his burial ("Three Blind Mice"?), I wonder how long one has to grieve before one can get another kitten. This time, I find myself thinking, I may get a golden tabby with a long, long tail. I don't need a cold, indifferent, unresponsive Manx again, that's for sure. I don't need a cat that won't come in the house and prefers to be torn limb from limb instead.

I get into my nightgown. I brush my teeth. I run to the front door and throw it open, expecting him to be at the dishes of sardines, gobbling away. But the dead little fish are still sitting there in their oily bowls. Soon ants will be swimming in them. It's hopeless.

I try to sleep but am inconsolable. I think of him out there in the dark: tiny, lost, helpless, pathetic, lonely, scrunched down in the dirt somewhere, wishing he were in my arms.

I suppose I fall asleep, but I don't feel as if I have, even when my eyes open in the morning. I leap out of bed and run to the back door. And there, there, curled tightly against Big Kitty, body to body, Maxie is sleeping on the lounge chair, safely at rest, the hunter home from the hill.

He hears me open the screen door. He looks up. Like a man who's had a late date, he hasn't much energy. But he rises slowly, stretches his long haunches, steps down from the chair, and trots expectantly toward me. He isn't going to make up, I can see that. He wants breakfast, but even more, he wants his morning greeting. I sit down on the step; he walks into my lap, walks up my chest with his front paws, and embraces me with the soft pads of his feet.

Okay, I love you too, I tell him with my eyes. *All is forgiven.*

April 28

I almost feel as if I could teach Maxie to speak to me. Sometimes he studies my face so closely, so carefully, that I feel he's straining to learn something just beyond his grasp, that he wants to know, to understand. If he's looking into my eyes, and I blink slowly, he makes a tiny sound, a bleep, a gentle combination of mew and cry, that tells me he's trying to comprehend, to say something that has no language. There are times he's wrapped himself sleepily into a warm circle on my lap, but isn't satisfied, isn't close enough, somehow. He climbs high upon me, settles over my heart, but even that isn't close enough, so he comes higher, toward my face, places his paws, like hands, on each of my shoulders, and brings his nose to my nose, his lips almost to my lips.

Sometimes Maxie notices that J., sitting beside me on the couch, is unattended, and uncoils himself and steps over to caress him. J. is always surprised, but more and more he's receptive, he makes room for Maxie, he places his big hand gently on Maxie's small head and strokes him, he lets Maxie curl in his lap and even holds him there, appreciative to be so chosen.

I feel flooded with love at these moments, as if the universe has come into harmony somehow, as if a peaceable kingdom can exist, as if our best instincts, our most gentle and loving capabilities, can rise up like blossoms and bloom one by one.

Maxie, like any adolescent, can only take so much of home and hearth; I see it happen over and over. Something seems suddenly to occur to him, a memory, an urge like a hunger. He leaps up and runs to the door. As quickly as that he's done with sweet love and soft touches. His muscles want to stretch, his senses want to confront the night—the high cold light of the moon, the crickets rasping in the bushes, the cloying perfume of jasmine, the jungle camouflage of brambles and thick foliage. I can do nothing to call him back, to convince him that the night is dangerous, that he's better off here in our warmth and company, that he'll only find trouble out there, in those tempting landscapes.

Try and tell that to any teenager; I told it often enough to my daughters. They went out anyway, they burst out of captivity to explore the universe, they avoided some traps, but fell into others. How craftily nature has designed life, with so many pleasures, so many dangers. Certain experiences reward us so fully that we're flagrant in our willingness to risk taking on the others.

But I can't ignore a need so desperate; can't deny Maxie his rightful will to hunt, to explore, to see the world on terms I will never know. (How often I have to tell this to myself. Like an old person, with limited short-term memory, I forget I have been this way before.)

Many times I have read and heard spoken the words: "We put the cat out for the night." Clearly it is done, and is an acceptable thing to do. Some night I will have to willingly do the same. It's true Maxie has already survived a night out, why not let him take on all nights? Why not begin tonight? Big Kitty has been living outside, day and night, for twelve years. Why can't Maxie be allowed to have this small night, a warm night, a peaceful night, without storm or wind, in his own backyard? Why not?

All right. He shall have it. And once given it, he won't find me out there like a mad housewife, dragging sausages and sardines to lure him back inside. I don't confer with J. since he's all too willing to have me cut the apron strings. Maxie has proven himself for nearly six months; he's come home, come in, come back to love me. This is the time to show my confidence. As if I'm giving the keys to the car to my child for the first time, I unlock the door and let Maxie out. He fairly flies out into the night, without hesitation, without caution. He disappears in the knitted mesh of shadows at the far end of the yard. I close the door and turn back to my inside, civilized life, wondering how I will be able to sleep the night.

~

Somewhere around midnight, I hear gunshots! Or automatic machine-gun fire. Or a car backfiring. Or possibly firecrackers, since the Fourth of July is only two months away. I throw off the covers and leap out of bed, my heart pounding. *Maxie,* I think. *He'll be terrified.* I grab my robe and rush outside. Where can he be? Where shall I look? Where to begin?

The night is foggy with low clouds; the moon is obscured, fuzzy, dim. I don't know where night creatures go in the night; I never know where Big Kitty sleeps, he has his secret hideaway, a place no one is permitted to discover, though some mornings I find him asleep on a patio chair, or on the pool heater grid, where the pilot light emits a steady warmth. I make my rounds of the house; the front yard, peering behind the camellia bushes and the mock orange trees; the side yard, peering behind the garbage cans, under the woodpile; the backyard, that great expanse (to Maxie) that provides jungle, meadow, bush, and veldt, all at once. As a last resort I try the pool area, which is fenced off and gated, and I look around its small concrete deck, look into the pool (heaven forbid!) and then, by chance, I glance at the screen that covers the crawl space opening. There, cowering against the rusted wire, is Maxie, back at the place of his origins, at the entrance to the cave in which I first found him crying for food and comfort.

I scoop him up in my arms and cover his face with kisses. "Oh Maxie, Maxie," I croon to him. "Too much night for such a little kitten, too many loud noises, too much black sky."

He doesn't protest. He licks the top of my hand, licks my cheek, is against me and all over me in happiness that he has been found again.

This time I take him back to bed with me. I hold him on my body, just until both of our heartbeats slow down, till we are warm and breathing slowly. Till he begins to purr, and then purrs deeply and then falls asleep, silent. Only then, when he is limp and relaxed, do I tiptoe with him to his bed in the laundry room, place him on his soft, deep pillow, and promise myself that it will be some time before I allow him another night out.

April 30

I haven't been to see my mother since Saturday night, the night she threw up and begged an aide to get her a clean gown, the night the aide said she was too busy, and when my mother buzzed the call bell incessantly, came back and threw a rolled-up hospital gown at her face and hit her with it. My mother begged me not to report it; she didn't know the aide's name, anyway. If she did, she wouldn't tell me, because she feared retaliation. "And I'm helpless and alone here, you know."

I find it harder and harder to go back to the nursing home, to summon the energy for the visit, to have to face what she lives with there, to go prepared, as if to perform a show, with a script to recite, with props to display, with a subtle exit line memorized and a plan to get off the stage gracefully, without making it too obvious, without having my feet sound loud on the hollow floor.

The thought that recurs to me is this: one day when I will want to see my mother and want it desperately, when I would give almost anything to be able to see her face, look into her burning eyes, hear her voice—one day that will no longer be possible. I know she will be dead soon, how soon I can't calculate, but she will be gone from me—all the signs point to her disappearance. Whereas tonight, a night in which I have nothing much to do, nothing of importance, nothing I will even remember doing a day or two from now, where-as tonight when I could go there now, drive there this *instant*, be there in less than ten minutes, whereas tonight *while she is still in the world,* I choose not to stir from my chair, I choose not to connect to her. Instead I decide to shower, wash my hair, watch some foolish TV program.

I feel as if I'm daring fate, as if I am waiting too long under a freeway underpass thinking, "The earthquake won't come this instant! I don't have to race to make the light and get through." At the same time I'm thinking, "If the earthquake comes, maybe I'll be crushed instantly and never know what hit me." Tonight I am playing that game: "She won't die tonight. She hasn't died any night up to now and she's eighty-five years old. That is, she has not died in 30,600 nights, why should she die tonight?" And yet this could be the night the fatal stroke takes place; this could be the night of the clot to the heart, to the lungs, to the vital brain. Something has to happen some night, some day; we are all turning on the wheel, irrevocably moving to that place from which we drop off and disappear.

She could die without warning; or, if she has warning, she could die without my being warned. The nurses might not call me until the news is real: your mother has stopped breathing. Your mother has had a stroke. Your mother is unconscious, we can't rouse her. Your mother. . . .

I begin to cry, because soon there will be no mother, no "your" mother, no "my mother," no one human being who has known me from the first day I drew breath, who loves me above all others, who would give her life for me. And I, I won't even put on my shoes and drive the five miles to see her because I don't want to feel afraid, while looking upon her face, that I will lose her.

≈

I go to see her first thing the next morning. I come laden with presents. Well, if not presents, exactly, at least I come laden with mints, with a teaspoon of honey to put on her tongue, and with a snapshot of my youngest daughter to put on the wall. Now that she has her new roommate, Naomi, who has a large framed portrait of her handsome young husband (long dead) on the little dresser, perhaps my mother might be tempted to display a photo of one of *her* relatives.

"I'm so happy to see you," she says. "When you're not here, there's no one to talk to, to tell about what's happening." I sit back for a long session. She begins: what's happening is not to be believed, how they ignore her, tell her "Later," or "I'm busy," or "I have to feed the other patients," or "I'll come back later." They never do. They forget the one small thing she wanted, some cream for her chapped lips, her bed elevated or flattened, the curtain pulled against the brilliant sunlight, the lumpy pillow smoothed under her head. "I hope I don't live to my eighty-sixth birthday, Merrill," she tells me.

Then she falls silent, exhausted by her effort to criticize the world, waiting for me to say I will try to set it right. I begin my presentation, wishing I had planned a better show. I change the subject without transition. I tell her about which appliances have broken lately, about the noise I heard outside that I thought might be gunshots or automatic machine-gun fire. I tell her about Maxie, his newest little adventure (how he came around to the front door with Big Kitty, who taught him that it was a good place to meow for food). I strain for information that might interest her: the latest scandal on a quiz show, the recession that is causing local libraries to close, the waves of crime, car-jackings, kidnappings. She tells me, "I don't want you to go out at night alone." I assure her I won't (although last week I did teach a night class, and had to park my car far away and was frightened when I had to walk through the darkened, empty parking lot to get into it).

The clock moves on; I glance at it, I have been here over an hour. How do I leave, how do I make my exit? My mother is so alert! She sees me checking the clock. She says, "What do you have to do when you leave here?"

"We're all out of food," I say, which is my standard ploy. "There's nothing in the house at all, not an egg, not a loaf of bread."

"Well, then, go!" she says, taking her cue. "Go right now before you get too tired." It seems we are both relieved to have reached the familiar place in the script.

"Okay," I admit. "I better go right now." And I stand up to leave her, leave her to stare at the wall, to ring her buzzer into the void, while I kiss her good-bye and am already out the door, rushing past the aides in white, walking fast, almost running in my blessed free-dom, driving fast to the supermarket, pushing my silver cart with determination, with strength, with pleasure, for once happy, no, not just happy, but *ecstatic*, to be lucky enough to be able to choose a let-tuce with brilliant green leaves, to tap for the hollow sound on the first watermelons of the season, to break off a bunch of bananas, to squeeze a few tomatoes, to pop the inside juice of a grape against my tongue before I choose a bunch that's sweet enough. But they're all sweet, every one of them, sweet to a person that's well, strong, standing on her own two feet, years and years from the nursing home . . . (as my grandmother used to say) God willing.

May 5

Cinco De Mayo at the nursing home. There is great activity when I arrive; balloons and crepe paper streamers are being strung across the central patio, aides are wheeling patients in their wheelchairs and getting them settled in one spot, locking the brakes, then going back to get another patient. I stop for a moment before I go inside to visit my mother; the waterfall in the goldfish pond has been turned on for the festivities; the rushing water makes a soothing sound. I see tables on wheels being pushed along on which are great tubs of ice cream as well as several sheet cakes, iced in green.

Today is a brilliant day; bright sun, a cool breeze, flowers on the patio in bloom, roses everywhere. The number of wheelchairs grows as I watch—I count thirty, fifty, eighty, and they are coming from every direction. Someone has wheeled the old upright piano to the center of the patio, and draped it with pink and yellow crepe paper.

I pull open the door to my mother's wing and find her alert and watching the door of her room as I walk in.

"You're just in time!" she says.

"That's good. For what?" I ask. I smile at her roommate as I pass her bed, and she smiles back at me.

"My TV doesn't work."

"It's just come unplugged," I tell her. I find the plug, plug it in.

"They don't care," she says. "They come in here with their brooms and they shove things around and they don't care what they break."

"Mom," I say. "They're having a Cinco de Mayo celebration outside in a few minutes. Why don't I have an aide put you in the wheelchair and I'll take you out?"

"I'm in no shape," she says. "What do I need that nonsense for? Noise. Commotion. I'd collapse." She begins to point out her pains. "I have them all across here all the time, but I can't remember what they are. Naomi reminds me."

"Peptic ulcer!" Naomi calls out gaily from her bed.

"I had the nurse write it down on my tissue box," my mother says. "But I can't even remember to look there. I can't remember anything."

"Think of Pepsi-Cola," I suggest. "Or Pepto-Bismol."

"What is peptic ulcer?" my mother asks me. I flinch, because what comes to mind is that a bleeding ulcer is what my mother's mother died of.

"It's just an inflammation of the stomach lining," I tell her. "Don't worry. You're getting medicine for it."

From outside we hear the music begin. "Mom," I say, "let me go out and see what's happening." I slide back her screen door and step outside, into sun, flowers, the sound of a waterfall. The aides seem so cheerful, chattering with one another, passing out bowls of ice cream and cake to the patients. The employees at the nursing home are primarily Mexican—this is their day, their holiday. The women wear colorful smocks and bright ribbons in their black hair, the male aides (those who work with the patients, in the kitchen, in the maintenance crew) are dressed in white; all are holding bowls filled with green cake and strawberry, vanilla, and chocolate ice cream.

There is a sea of white hair as far as I look in every direction; there must be three hundred patients outside here today. As the aides walk among them, adjusting their wheelchair positions, their blankets and restraints, sometimes touching them lovingly on the arm, or smoothing their hair, I realize that despite this attention they give, the old people are secondary to their real life that goes on here, the meetings and assignations, the flirtations, the animated gossip of the young girls, the plotting whispers of the men, the conspiracies, the intrigues. In a sense, the nursing home is a great dating service for these young people; they seem not to be affected by the certainties of living long, of what will befall them if they survive to a great old age.

I sit down on a bench in the sun, and let my glance land on face after face of the very old. So many faces, so many diminished lives! Here is a regal woman with long white hair in two handsome braids; there is another with a beautiful profile, her head held high; a man with a shock of thick white hair, who, if he stood, must be over six feet tall; there—a petite woman with her hair in a ballerina's bun. What time and care the aides take to groom their patients; so much kindness and respect is evident in their behavior (even if sometimes, as my mother swears, there is abuse, also).

I go back into my mother's room and beg her to come outside. She waves me away; she has no time for a party at this point in life. The nurse comes in to treat the recently infected feeding tube incision; she swabs my mother's pale belly with disinfectant and replaces the bandages.

"Ah," she says, as strains of the music outside drift into the room. "We used to have a beautiful magician, Amado, play for us with his mariachi band."

"Musician," my mother corrects her.

"No," the nurse says dreamily. "He was a magician. He would play and we'd be in Mexico, we'd be at a fiesta, we'd all be dancing, and not here, in these halls."

"What happened to him?" I ask.

"Oh, he started playing in clubs. He became famous, I think, and he never came back here."

The nurse, whose name is Maria (one of a thousand Marias who work here) tells me she misses Amado. She sighs, and, leaning over my mother, fluffs her pillow.

"Surely you must go out and have some ice cream and cake," I say. "Everyone is out there."

"Oh, later, maybe," she says. "I have to put pills in cups for so many . . ."

From outside we hear the sound of a tambourine. I push back the screen door and step outside. A mysteriously beautiful woman, swathed in veils, is moving barefoot over the patio. On her upper arms are golden bracelets in the shape of snakes; around her hips she wears a cascade of coins which shimmer and buzz with every step she takes. She pauses briefly at a tape player on one of the tables and pushes a button; music—rich with the sound of drums and eastern string instruments—fills the air. I know this music—it wasn't all that long ago that I danced to it.

"Mom!" I call back into my mother's room. "There's a belly dancer out here. Remember when I used to take belly-dance lessons? Remember when I made myself a costume, and made costumes for the children, too?"

"I don't really remember," she says. "My mind is going."

"Yes," I insist. "You must remember! You came to see me dance at the park when we gave a performance!"

"Maybe I did. Who knows?" she says.

Just as she says this, the belly dancer comes shimmying along the patio walk and shakes her coins in front of my mother's room. "You must come out and join the party," she calls in, rattling her tambourine.

"That's my mother inside," I say.

"Well, Mother, come on out!" she says, and—as she looks at me—I see that I know her.

"Nancy!" I cry. "You were my teacher! At the Rec Center! Didn't you teach belly dance there a long time ago?"

"Yes, I did. I *thought* you looked familiar to me."

"It must be twenty years ago!" I say. "I took your class while my kids were taking origami lessons one summer."

"Well, we don't have to let these folks know exactly how old I am, do we?"

"To them you're still a teenager!" I say. "We both are!"

"Do you still belly dance?" she says.

"Only when no one is home," I admit.

"Then come on . . . help me out here. I often dance at this place. Come out and join me."

"What's going on?" my mother demands.

"There's a party going on! And you should be at it. Your daughter is going to dance for everyone." Nancy, my old teacher, looks at the nurse Maria and says, "Can't you put her in the wheelchair and bring her out?"

"If she wants to go, sure," Maria says.

"She wants to," the belly dancer says. She stares at my mother and says, "Don't you? I'm sure you want to. I'm taking your daughter with me, but you be outside in two minutes, and you'll have a surprise."

Nancy grabs my hand and pulls me with her. My mother is too astonished to serve up all her arguments.

~

Five minutes later I am wrapped in an iridescent veil. I have zills on my fingers to tap out a rhythm, and a coin belt jangles over my hips. In no time I am busy doing the moves my body remembers: the hip-lift, the figure eight, the camel-walk. It all comes back like the knowledge of any bodily art: like bike riding, like roller-skating.

Nancy pulls me with her to the center of the circle of old people, she introduces me as the daughter of one of the residents. She announces that I am going to dance with her . . . and we begin. I am laughing so hard I can barely see in front of me. I sway and bend, I shake and shimmy. I click my zills. I wish J. were here to see this!

I can't believe I've been talked into this, but it's such a pleasure to be dancing! To be laughing! And here, at this place, of all places.

I know the old people won't be judging me harshly. Half of them are asleep in their wheelchairs, the rest can't see very well, and those who are watching are laughing with me.

As I move, following my teacher, I see my mother being wheeled into the circle by her nurse. I see my mother's dear face, framed by her white hair. I see her glancing around, trying to find me among the crowd.

I am filled with a powerful sense of joy, like a child in a first-grade play who feels strong, confident, and safe because her mother has waved to her from the audience.

"Here I am, Mom. Over here! Your dancing girl!"

My mother smiles. It's a strange, soft, poignant smile, a smile without teeth, a smile that's half a cry. But it *is* a smile, there's no mistaking it. My mother and I are at a party together. We are sharing time in a place where there's life, laughter, and music. I wouldn't have believed such a moment was still possible, miracle that it is. I feel myself laughing till tears stand in my eyes. "Hey, Mom," I cry as I dance past her. "Look at me! Look at me!"

May 7

Now when Maxie sees daylight, he begins to cry from his room. Instead of greeting me from his basket and licking my face in happiness, he is already on the floor of the laundry room and at the door, ready to run out as I slide it open. If I don't show immediate signs of popping open his can of food, he nips my ankles to remind me, and then races ahead of me to the sliding door to the backyard. Only after he has eaten most of his meal does he remember he hasn't had a proper greeting, and begins to cry to come back in the house and into my lap.

Today we are having *matzo brie* (matzo soaked in egg and fried in butter). As J. and I talk about the latest round of senseless shootings in today's paper, Maxie floats up into my lap in one of those effortless leaps, and looks at the remains of breakfast on the table. My plate is empty, but J. has a few crumbs left on his. "Have you anything for Maxie?" I ask, and J. places a crumb in his palm and holds it out. Maxie puts his front paws on the table and begins to eat the food from J.'s open palm.

I feel oddly and excessively pleased at this shared gesture between them, it makes me want to hug Maxie and J.—and I do, quite suddenly, both at the same time. This is the effect that Maxie's living here tends to have on me; I am flooded with tenderness because he is trusting and sweet, and because J. responds to Maxie in a way he has never been able to respond to any animal before. Maxie seems to have that capability, to awaken tenderness and warmth in both of us.

~

Someone, my mother says the instant I arrive, has broken her TV. Not just unplugged it with a sudden sweep of a broom, or moved it out of reach, but smashed the transformer and plug. "You're just in time," she says. (Yes! Yes! I know!)

"Don't worry. We'll get it fixed. We'll have it all fixed up."

"I don't care," she says. "I'm sick and tired of TV. I'm sick and tired of everything." I don't invite her to elaborate. I am sharpening my technique for making sudden turns, for changing the direction of her thoughts. I open the plastic bag containing her light robes that I've washed, now all fragrant and folded. We examine them together as I put them in the closet: I describe each one as if I am writing copy for a fashion magazine. "See? This is your blue flowered one, this is the one with the orange patch pocket . . ."

"I don't have a warm jacket," she says. "What if I have to go out?"

"Go out?"

We look at one another. I say, "I'll bring you a jacket next time I come."

"Bring me an old one of yours," she says. "I don't need anything fancy."

There's no need for me to call attention to the logical implications her remark brings to mind. I return to taking inventory of the closet: how many hangers, how many sweaters. Then we check the currently used robes in the top drawer (clean), the ones in the bottom drawer (soiled). She always tells me she doesn't think this one or that one is hers; she doesn't remember having a robe of that blue color, or that pink. "They're all yours," I reassure her. "I bought you every one of them."

"Maybe they belong to some dead old lady."

"No, Mom," I tell her. "They're all yours, they belong to you—an alive old lady."

"How long do I have to be alive?"

"No one knows these things, Ma."

"Close the drapes," she says. "People passing by can see me in here, and one of these days someone will walk by and shoot and kill me."

"Well, if you're shot, then you're out of here, Mom," I say, smiling to indicate it's a joke. "You won't be alive. Just what you want."

But she is not amused today. She wants to tell me about her pains. She insists she needs an enema. The nurses say they're too busy to give her one. They're always too busy. One threatened to take away her call bell if she rang it one more time.

"Let me see what I can do," I say. "Let me talk to the charge nurse."

I'm eager to leave her room, to let down for a minute, to move out of the magnetic field of her relentless demands, questions, requirements. I stand in the hall for a minute to catch my breath. Then I walk over to the nurses' station. I know all the women there, the nurses' aides, the social service aide, the charge nurse, the physical therapist. They are busy writing in charts, getting medications ready, making phone calls. In the background I hear the constant screaming of a man. I apologetically request an enema for my mother.

The charge nurse says, "Oh yes, Jessie." She looks up the standing orders on her chart. Yes, it says Jessie may have an enema on request. Yes, this will be possible, she will see that it's done shortly.

"Your mother, how come she wants attention all the time?" the aide says to me. "She has so much fear. She rings the bell every minute. I tell her, 'Wait, Jessie, I'm on break now,' but no, she has to have something that very minute."

"I'm sorry," I say. "It's the way she is." I *am* sorry. I am sorry for them. I am sorry for myself.

I rush back to her room. "You'll have your enema," I tell her. "The nurse is coming right in with it."

"That's what she says, but I could wait a year."

Just then the nurse does appear with her little plastic enema bottle and draws the curtain around my mother's bed.

"Mom, you don't need me here for this?" I ask her, almost pleading. "Do you?"

I know she would prefer to have me witness what follows, have me stand as witness to every aspect of her pain, but she must hear what's in my voice. "No, I don't need you," she says.

She doesn't need me! I feel like a racehorse at the starting post. I tear out of there, excused, free. I am always racing away, fast, before they lasso me, pull me in, put me in *my* designated bed. It's no surprise to me how often I see my own face on that pillow, imagine my own fate, a mere thirty years from now.

On the way home I see, on a street corner, two Mexican girls selling flats of fresh, ripe strawberries—brilliant, red, enormous.

I must have some! I desire them with a fierce need for their fragrance, for their beauty, for the sun glittering on their vivid skins. I pull my car over and set the brake.

"How much?" I call.

"Five dollars," one of them says. I would pay more, I think. I would pay a ransom for them! I take the cardboard flat in my arms like a baby, and set it gently on my front seat. All the way home (and I speed home, I fly home!) I inhale their perfume, their seedy, earthy scent. And the instant I get into the kitchen, I fling a handful under water, rinse them, and gobble them up, one after another. Seeing my mother has made me feel parched and shriveled; I take in the fruit like a benediction.

May 20

Maxie seems to have abandoned me. I have seen it coming, but this is total rebellion. He insists on staying out late or won't come home at all. When he returns, he drops no hint as to where he's been. He refuses to listen when spoken to, nor does he come when called. In fact, when I call him, he tends to turn tail (small tail that it is) and run the other way. I think he may even eat elsewhere from time to time, since he occasionally turns up his nose at the shrimp/salmon entree or the liver/chicken minced grill I set down, tastefully arranged on a dish for him.

Do I feel hurt? Well, I am not ignorant of the ways of the world, but this seems to have happened so fast! With my children, the leave-taking was protracted: they were babies for years, babies still at two and three, baby-like even to age six or seven, and by eleven or twelve still showed signs of childlike dependency, neediness, even offered up flares of urgent affection.

But with Maxie the change has taken place in only a matter of months. I haven't properly prepared myself. His teenage hostility cuts me to the quick.

Last night I found the severed head of a small bird on the patio. Its eye (the one turned toward me) was already hollowed by ants. I assume this killing was the work of Maxie (I think Big Kitty is too sluggish, too spoiled by easy-gotten nourishment to bother with live game). But certainly Maxie is through with his toys; he shuns the parrot with the grass skirt, the killer shoulder-pad on a string, the rolling Ping-Pong ball. He has graduated to the real thing. His "catness" has asserted itself. And why shouldn't it? He is, after all, in his deepest heart, a cat.

$\sim$

In the evening there is a documentary on the public television station called, "Good-bye and Goodnight," about the dying days of an old Jewish woman, filmed by her granddaughter. The old woman has the look of my mother, the look (perhaps) of any gaunt, ill-nourished, ancient woman in the last months of her life. I am drawn to watch it, but I don't want to be alone. (J. is in his study, working on the papers on his desk.)

I decide to capture Maxie; the need to do so is so fierce, my field of determination so intense, that he has no time to duck me when I find him on the patio. I swoop him up in my arms, hearing the silly tinkle of the little bell I attached to his collar (the better to find him at night), hearing his slightly protesting meow. But he doesn't struggle much; he may have begun to be bored by the outside entertainments of the evening; he seems willing, even agreeable, to have my attention lavished upon him.

I take him to the couch and lie down, arranging him upon my breast. He seems to remember our old attachment; he extends his paw to stroke my cheek, climbs higher upon me to press his nose into the curve of my neck. Aah, perhaps he is mine again for these few minutes.

I turn my attention to the documentary and see the predictable, familiar pain on the faces of family members as they view the old dying woman (diabetes, cancer) as they visit with her, talk with her, make gefilte fish with her, ask her about her romance with her long-dead husband ("Who can remember?" she says. "It was so long ago.")

Last week my own mother asked me if she'd ever met J.'s mother. "Ever met her?" I'd said. "My mother-in-law? You met her thousands of times." "I don't remember," my mother said. "What did she look like? I hardly remember anything."

"Do you remember your mother and father?" I was prepared to be horrified. But she said, "Of course I do. Of course I remember them."

On the screen I see what I know so well; the diminishment of a beloved person; her slipping, slipping away, her visible suffering, her weakness, her loosening grip on life and what used to be important to her. And the children and grandchildren look on in horror; one grandson asserts that she doesn't deserve this kind of suffering; what has she done in her life that is evil or vicious? What kind of logic or justice could produce this end to an ordinary, average, mundane existence? What sense can one make out of it?

I, too, have had this thought, looking at my mother; the hours, days, *months*, of pain she has endured; the shocks to her poor body, the broken wrist and shoulder of several years ago, the more recent attack of shingles, the stroke, the broken hip. I remember how—just one day after the hip was broken, when they had her legs in contracting plastic sleeves that squeezed hard every few seconds to expedite circulation through the limbs—she cried out: "Take them off, it hurts, it hurts." What *hasn't* hurt her? The waking up one morning with the realization that the use of her right hand was gone: was this not cruel and unusual punishment? The hideous smashing of her hip socket after the terrible fall; can any person account, in any possible way, for her having *deserved* such a denouement to a long life of labor, dedication to family, and struggle? And if there's no reason to any of this, how do we account for reason at all? For the idea of trials and rewards? For struggle and accomplishment? For good works and the benefits that grow out of them?

There is hardly a crime that merits this kind of suffering; no serial killer struggles in pain for longer than a few seconds in the electric chair; no rapist writhes in leg chains like those plastic sleeves that squeezed my mother's legs, over and over, day after day.

I don't get it. I feel cheated, somehow, by the unfairness of the cosmic plan.

Maxie, snuggled against my chest, repositions himself, and presses his moist nose against my cheek. I am overcome by the trusting weight of his warm body, by the silken pleasure of his fur, by the earthy fragrance of his scent, tempered slightly by a pungent whiff of salmon entree (he has eaten the dinner I provided today, despite the bird he dismembered). I am alive and grateful to feel what I feel at this moment. Even if there is no rational cosmic plan, we do have, when we have it, this, this . . . *extreme* pleasure.

On the screen there is an imaginary procession of all the film-maker's friends and beloved people through the proverbial tunnel to the light at the end which is death. And in their place I suddenly imagine my own people, those already dead, and those on their way, which includes all of us: I see my father, walking in his slow, relaxed way, and I see my mother, with her high heels and her skirt swinging, and I see my in-laws, with their special gaits, and my aunt, taking small, mincing steps. I see myself and J., arm in arm, walking toward the light, and our three children; I see my sister, tall and walking alone; I see Beloved Korky, his tail high in the air, waiting to meet us on the other side; I see Big Kitty and Maxie making their cautious way over this unfamiliar territory.

I burst into tears—here on the couch, in the dark, with Maxie against my beating heart. He senses my breakdown, nuzzles the channel of tears on my cheek, climbs up me, against me, toward me till he is mouth to mouth with me. Someday we must let go of all we love. The truth tolls in my soul. Even Maxie, this precious little kernel of energy and natural joy, will wear out his days on earth. Who can bear it? Who ever could?

May 21

Just as I am about to cook dinner, a call comes from the nursing home to say that my mother is losing her hearing and says she needs to see me at once. My fingers are sticky with onion juice; my eyes are obscured by onion-tears. I tell J. to take out the roast in an hour and I drive the five miles to the nursing home.

Another chop of the axe, I think. Old age is chopping her down like a tree: the fruit, the leaves, the big branches, the little twigs, the trunk. But the roots hold fast, tenacious, dug in to life like claws. I have seen Maxie cling for dear life by his claws. Those few times I have tried to put him in his carry-case for a trip to the vet he has hung on to anything (myself included) rather than be stuffed in that box, hung on with super-strength, with pure willpower. That box: we don't want to know it. We never want to see the inside of it.

The streets seem oddly deserted for this rush-hour time; all the lights are green for me. It's as if the sea is parting to let me get there fast.

A ball game is going on at the park across the street from the nursing home and there are no parking spaces. I drive around to the back of the building and pass the outside patio where my mother used to sit . . . when she could walk, when she could eat, when she could hear. And in those days she thought of herself as incapacitated—no longer able to live alone, to drive, to shop, to cook, to be a human citizen. How does she think of herself now?

In the hallway I hear the usual screams: the old man who calls out "Help! Help!" all hours of the day, the woman who sobs, "I want my Mama, I want my Mama." The nurses at their station write away on their records, appearing to hear none of this. They may be immune by now.

In my mother's room, two TVs are turned on to *Jeopardy*. Her roommate, Naomi, watches on a big color TV, my mother observes the small black and white screen of the little portable, which we have had repaired.

"Ma," I say. "Hello, Ma."

She stares at the screen.

"Mom, it's me. Hi Mom. How are you, Mom?"

"She can't hear," Naomi tells me. "At three in the morning she turned on her TV and woke me up. So loud—she can't hear it so she makes it as loud as it goes."

"Ma!" I move into her line of sight, and she looks at me.

"Have you been here long? When did you come?"

"I just came," I say.

"What?" she says.

"I JUST CAME."

"Something is wrong with me," she says. "Maybe I had another stroke. I can't seem to hear anything."

I feel my heartbeat pause. I realize I'm not sure I believe her. For days she has been complaining that Naomi plays her TV too loud. Now I suspect (how ugly it is to be suspicious) that she is pretending to be hard of hearing in order to have a legitimate reason to turn up the volume of her TV to the highest level. But then—how come she didn't hear me arrive? How come (is she that good a plotter, an actress?) she didn't turn her head at the sound of my voice?

Naomi is trying to explain to me, in her stroke-mangled diction, how my mother seems to be suddenly hard of hearing. "And the other morning she woke me up and said to me, 'Where am I? Why am I here?'"

"Really?" I say to her.

"Your mother makes complaints against me, that I play my TV too loud. She has a chip on her shoulder, I don't know why."

"She was born with it there," I explain. "It's not your fault."

"I'd like to help her," she says. "I'd help her in any way I could."

"What? What?" my mother calls to me. "What is she saying?"

"Naomi says she'd like to help you if she could."

"She!" my mother spits out, scornful. "What could *she* do for me?"

"Maybe nothing, but she'd like to help." I excuse myself from the argument and go sit beside my mother. The feeding machine grinds on its circular path, the catheter tube extends beyond her sheets; its bag, half filled with urine, is at my feet. ("I never know when I'm going or not," my mother says each time I see her. "I don't know if I'm a person or a machine.")

I pull the orange plastic chair closer to her bed.

"So now I'm going deaf," she says to me. "What else is there to happen? What else have I got to lose?"

I note that my mother, like myself, jumps from a small bit of information to a fatal pronouncement. With us, it's all or nothing. We don't believe in increments of truth, of evidence, of the laying out of a detailed, well-reasoned proof.

"Maybe it's only ear wax," I say.

She doesn't want to hear it. She has already moved herself into this new dimension.

"I wish I were dead," she says. "I want to die." Her eyes seek mine. "I say it often because it's true. But the other day, maybe I said it once too often, and *she* . . ." (she motions toward Naomi) ". . . *she* began saying it, too. Over and over—'I wish I were dead, I wish I were dead.'"

"That's because I got sick of it," her roommate calls over to us. "How much do I have to listen to that?"

"What's she saying?" my mother demanded of me, her eyes angry.

"Just that it was hard for her to hear you say that, over and over. Remember, Ma, she's dealing with her own troubles. She can't walk. She lost most of her speech when she had her stroke."

"What?"

I repeat the sentence. (We are all talking above the noise of *Jeopardy* on TV.)

"Well," my mother dismisses that Naomi has troubles. "She's much better off than I am. At least she can be pushed around in her wheelchair."

"So can you!" I say loudly.

"No, I have to stay attached to this feeding tube."

"They can disconnect you, Ma. And if you wanted to eat on your own, you wouldn't even have to have a feeding tube."

"I can't chew, I can't wear my teeth."

"They would give you pureed food . . ." I stop short. We have been over this ground a million times. She doesn't remember or it doesn't matter to her that we have. Life has turned into these words, repeated over and over between us, like a ritual.

"Merrill," she whispers. "I don't want to live anymore. How can I get out of it?"

"I don't know, Mom."

"If only I could get out of it."

"It's a long wait for this bus, isn't it, Mom?"

"Too long," she says. Her eyes lock onto mine. "Is there any way?" Then she adds, "I know you can't do it."

"I could," I say. I have read *Final Exit*, I read Betty Rollins' book about how she helped her mother to die, I belong to the Hemlock Society.

"You don't have poison!" my mother says.

"I could find out how to get it."

"No," she says, with finality. "It would be too hard on your conscience." But at least I have opened the door for her to ask. Not that I could respond, or would, or would want to. I just want to know how desperate her need is.

"I don't want to live till I'm eighty-six," she says. "I don't want to live another night. I really mean it."

"I know, Ma." We are speaking in whispers, now. How can she hear me?

"I'm reading your lips," she says, as if she's reading my mind. "I can't hear you."

"Ma," I say. "There's a roast in the oven at home. I have to get home before it burns."

"You didn't eat dinner?"

"No."

"You should have eaten dinner first. Go home now. Eat."

"I will, Ma. I'll go home now."

"How will I know what will happen?"

"About what?"

"About my hearing."

"I'll call your doctor in the morning, Ma. I'll call the administrator of the nursing home tomorrow. We'll get a doctor to look at your ears, test them."

"I can hardly see, I can't eat, I can't walk, I can't use my hand, and now I can't hear."

"I know, Ma. I know."

"This is no good," she says.

And I think, *But we are here, you and I, in this life. And you are the one that brought me into it.*

June 3

Maxie now comes to me in a shimmering shower of bells. Since we are a good distance from the season of his December arrival on my doorstep (so to speak), I thought it safe to affix to his collar a small silver bell of the sort that is often attached to a ribbon-bedecked package. Now, when I call—and when he chooses to come—he travels over the grass toward me like a flying gift, ringing out his arrival. However, when he decides *not* to come flying, the bell is doubly useful to me. I stand still in the dewy night, under a gauzy moon, and repeat his name. Then I listen, my ears standing at attention like Maxie's. Even if he's chosen to hide (he still likes to play games with me at night, running the other way if he sights me) I can tell, at least, if he's there, hiding under a bush, or crouched in a tree branch. I know him by his silver tinkle.

The truth is that I no longer require him to come in for the night; I have more confidence now in his savvy, in his worldliness. If he wishes to ride the night out under cobwebs and moonbeams, listening to the rustling leaves and hiding from raccoons and possums, it's his right.

Privately, I think these nights on the town take their toll on him; often in the morning I find him crouched on the doormat, sleepy, but not sleeping. I get the sense that he has spent the night on guard, a lookout for his own safety, alert and tense. When I let him in the house, he falls asleep, almost at once, in a loose, trusting heap, either tucked against the back of the couch, his legs flung wide and open, or in a tight warm ball sunk into the cushion of a chair.

～

Tonight I watch the Frederick Wiseman film *Zoo*, another in a series of this filmmaker's extraordinary documentaries. Having a new and urgent interest in animals myself, I hold my breath as I watch the pregnant rhino deliver her baby, watch as the zoo veterinarians work over the calf, doing CPR, clearing mucus from its mouth, tapping its nostrils, breathing into its nose, then admitting its stillborn reality. I hold my breath, also, as they dissect the body, cut off its head, pull out its organs, toss the remainder into the zoo crematorium.

This is no film for the tender-hearted; rather, the tender-hearted need buttressing. I go outside and find Maxie, and hold him in my arms as I watch the rest of it. When gazelles are shown found torn to bits by wild pit bulls (one dog is shot by zoo employees and joins the rhino baby in the incinerator), I stroke Maxie's whole, complete, healthy body in gratitude. I feel I should cover his eyes when a wolf is shown being castrated by a female vet with two female assistants. I think back on Maxie's ordeal by knife, seeing now—in living color—the blood and sinew, bandages and sutures I was spared seeing when Maxie had his surgery.

I am not all that faint-hearted, but I cringe when a young woman takes a white rabbit out of his cage, holds him upside down, asking "Are you ready?" and then whacks him senseless with an iron rod before feeding him whole to a boa constrictor, who takes him down in one grotesque swallow.

Oh, Maxie! I think, showering his silken head with kisses, aware of the dangers in the world, full of gratitude that for one more night we have escaped them.

～

My mother, too, has escaped (for once) a swipe of the scythe. She is not deaf, she is not even losing her hearing. More than a week after her terror, a doctor finally comes to the nursing home, looks into her ears, cleans them with a syringe and restores to her the prime sense of communication.

When I visit I find her sitting beside her bed in her wheelchair, almost jolly. She actually says, "I am so grateful. I can hear your voice." I sit close to her and we talk and talk, we relish this most ordinary thing we are doing, exchanging words. I tell her about what's happening at home (the new place mats I bought for the circular glass table in the kitchen . . . Becky on jury duty . . . Maxie learning that the front door leads into our house as well as the back door). From down the hall we hear the anguished but usual cries of the patients: "Where's my momma?" "Help me, I need help!" For once my mother doesn't say, "That goes on all the time. How can a person stay sane in this place?" She says, instead, "I couldn't even hear *that* a few days ago! Now I can hear it!"

How quickly, indeed, we become grateful for small blessings. Out of the blue, she says, "I think I need a haircut, Merrill."

"Then why don't we do one?" I am down the hall in a second, asking at the nursing station for a pair of scissors and a sheet to act as an apron.

One of the aides sees me setting up: I wet my mother's hair with a wet hairbrush, I make a part in the wild white fan of her long hair. "Oh, Yessie," she calls. "You are so lucky to have your daughter."

"Yes, I'm lucky to have this daughter," she says. Naomi wakes up and watches us. Although she's had a stroke, her vanity has remained unscathed. Her hair has been done recently: cut, styled, permanented. She is in favor of this for my mother. Two of the nurses who work in this wing stop by to watch me cut and snip. The scissors are none too good; in fact, this pair is an angled arrangement used for cutting off casts, I think, but it will have to do.

How white my mother's hair is—like angel hair. How fine. How soft. The delicate nape of her neck is soft as a baby's skin. My beautiful mother.

I cut it short, severe. "No curls for me," she says. "Be sure to thin it out. I don't like those fluffy wigwams that people wear on their heads these days."

"I'm making you look like a fashion model, Ma," I say. "Sleek, like a seal."

"Just so you don't make me look like a rat."

Laughter. I hear laughter in the nursing home. There is life here, too.

"I haven't looked in a mirror in a year," my mother says. "I wouldn't know myself if I fell over myself."

"Let me get the little mirror I have on my key chain," I tell her, and I retrieve it from my purse. I hold the tiny circle up to my mother's eyes. She stares hard, looking for that mother who is thirty, forty, fifty years younger.

"You look beautiful, Yessie," Elena, the aide says to her. "Just beautiful, like a queen."

"Thank you," she says, but there is terror in her eyes. To me she adds, "My face scares me. That isn't me, Merrill. That old hag isn't me."

~

When I get home there is a message on the answering machine from the nursing home. In a routine examination, the nurse has found that my mother's feeding tube opening is infected, most likely with a staph germ; it's draining. It's a highly contagious organism. They are going to have to put her in isolation, in another room, and anyone entering will have to wear gloves, a mask, and a white coat.

June 7

I suit up like an astronaut to visit my mother: a long-sleeved gown with elastic at the wrists, rubber gloves, a mask. A red sign posted at her door warns of infection, precautions, danger, death. Just inside the door to her room are two enormous red barrels, one for infectious waste and one for infectious laundry. In the midst of all these alarms is my pale, quiet mother, getting more invisible every day, propped on her white pillows, the outlines of her new short haircut lost, white against white.

"I thought I was dreaming," she said. "I thought I heard your voice out in the hall."

"You did," I say. "I was asking the nurse if I had to wear all this stuff, the gown and gloves." I am talking through the mask hooked over my ears by two loops of string. I feel my own breath warming my lips, heating my face on an already hot June day.

"I know your voice," my mother says.

"You know my voice, Mom. You know it better than anyone."

"It made me happy just to hear it."

Again I feel a wild pang of fear for the loss that's coming. The rules that are not negotiable are posted in my mind like the red sign in my mother's doorway. One day (this is where the fear is at its highest pitch) there will be no mother on earth for me to visit. It's that simple. I can search forever in the red-posted rooms in every nursing home in the universe; she won't be there.

I sit down at the foot of her bed and touch her foot under the sheet.

"Don't touch me, they think I'm dangerous."

"It's just your feeding tube incision that's infected, Mom, and you're on antibiotics. I don't think there's any danger to me."

"What else will go wrong next?" my mother asks. It's a perfectly logical, perfectly simple question. She doesn't know I lie awake nights asking myself this. What is the next emergency-to-come? Another stroke, which will render her speechless and trapped inside her body? Another fall? (Only if someone drops her!) Heart attack then? Claudication of the blood vessels (I have only just recently learned this word)? Blood clot to the lungs? Bleeding ulcer? Cancer? What about that sweet deliverance we've all read about, dying in one's sleep? Does it happen anymore? And to whom?

"I'd like to see the doctor," my mother says.

"Why? Is something wrong?" (I can't believe how one can ask such foolish questions.)

"I'd like to see Dr. Kevorkian," she says. "Dr. Death."

"He wouldn't take you on, Mom. You don't have a fatal illness. You're not terminal."

"Then what would you call me?" She gestures around her, to the full extent of her existence, the feeding tube machine, and the five-inch TV on her tray table.

It seems to me we have covered this territory before, but here we are again. It's either her bowels we talk about, or the metaphysical state of her existence; there appears to be no middle ground. And we always get right to it, don't we?

I search my mind for things I can tell her: what I bought at a garage sale recently, or what I cooked, or what I cleaned in the house, or what I planted in the backyard, or what news I have from friends or relatives to relay to her.

"Oh," I say, glad to remember something. "Your friend Fred, he phoned to ask how you are. And he told me something he said to relay to you: that years ago, when he wrote his will, he willed you all his records and music upon his death."

"Is he dead?" my mother asks.

"No, he's alive. But he thought you might be happy to know that."

"I'm happy," my mother says. She closes her eyes.

I am aware of how hot my fingers are in the rubber gloves; my hands are burning. I am sweating all over, in the long-sleeved gown, under the mask on my face.

"You know," she says, "I turn the TV on and off a thousand times a day. I'm so bored; I'm bored to death. I wish I *could* be bored to death. I have no control over anything, except turning the TV on and off. I say it to myself and I say it out loud: *I wish I were dead.*"

"Why do you say it, Ma?"

"Because it's true."

So here we are again, we've come full circle. What can I offer her? I say, "I have to go shopping. I have to buy cat food for Maxie."

"See?" she says. "If you didn't have to come here to see me, you'd have more time for Maxie."

"I like to come here to see you. It makes me happy to know I can see you."

"I'm a burden."

"No, Ma. Maybe if I had to take care of you myself, that would be very hard. But knowing that you're well cared for makes it possible for me to have these nice visits with you."

"When is your anniversary?" she asks abruptly.

"This month. June 23rd."

"I try to remember everyone's birthday, everyone's anniversary, everyone's phone numbers, everyone's addresses. I try to remember when you and your sister graduated from high school, when your children were born, what schools you went to, the names of your teachers. I go deep into the past, but I've forgotten almost everything. I dig up my mind. I have only my mind."

"It's a good mind, Mom. You gave me good stuff."

"I gave you good stuff," she says with satisfaction.

We hear a loud banging from the hall. I see the nurse, already gowned and gloved to enter, hammering pills to powder on a pounding board.

"Is she wearing her cap and gown?" my mother says.

I smile at her mistake. "Yes, she's getting your medicine ready."

The nurse approaches and begins her ministrations. She unplugs the feeding tube from the machine that dispenses high-calorie liquid food from an upside-down bottle, and uses a wide plastic syringe to suck up my mother's pulverized pills which are dissolved in liquid. Then she squirts the medicine from the syringe into the open end of the feeding tube.

"I don't have to swallow pills anymore," my mother says, with some satisfaction.

"Good, that's good," I say.

"I wish I could have an enema," she says to the nurse.

"We'll see," the nurse says. "I have to check your chart."

"I think I'm going now, Ma, to the store to get Maxie cat food."

"Good-bye," she says. She turns back to the nurse, to continue her negotiations. Intent on business, she has already forgotten I am there.

June 8

My mother has been in the nursing home for two years today. I have probably visited there six hundred times, plotting my route to stop (either when going to or coming from a visit) at the supermarket or the library or the thrift shop or the egg farm. The egg farm sells white eggs and brown eggs, fertile eggs and cracked eggs, super-jumbo eggs and peewee eggs. Sometimes when I stop there I stand at the glass viewing window and watch the eggs ride along the conveyor belts, watch them being scrubbed and rinsed, sorted and boxed. A team of young Mexican girls efficiently takes care of business—discarding broken eggs, sorting sizes. There is a candling room to the side where the eggs pass over a bank of brightly burning bulbs. The special eggs in which life has visibly begun are separated from the rest.

So many eggs! So many oval white perfect offerings, so much matter created in the service of life. Sometimes I am overwhelmed by the excess—so many eggs, so many chickens, so many babies in the world. So many old people. So many who have already died—so many dying now. I am capable of extreme emotion these days under the most ordinary circumstances. I see eggs, and I miss my mother in advance. I see eggs and tears fill my eyes. I buy eggs and cradle them against my breast on the way to the car, for fear they will fall and crack on the cement.

I have taken to buying the peewee eggs (three dozen for ninety-nine cents) as treats for Maxie and Big Kitty. Their eyes light up when I show them an egg; instinctively, they are alert, hungry, passionate for eggs. They must dream egg-shaped dreams, they must fantasize adventures of upsetting birds' nests, claiming the trophies—succulent, oozing, delicious, golden-yolked eggs.

I crack the eggs before their eyes, one in each bowl; Maxie gets his own egg, Kitty gets his own egg. They tend to check each other's bowls—perhaps to see whose egg is bigger. To verify that they're being treated equally.

Kitty suspects he is the loser. His expression these days is petulant. If a cat can frown, he seems to have perfected the expression. He hears me ringing the bell (which Maxie responds to from the far corners of the yard) and turns sullenly to watch for the dashing figure of Maxie. Maxie always comes, ears pointed, in his little bunny-gallop. He's happy to see Kitty; he nuzzles his nose. He chops at his tail. He loves Kitty. However, Kitty is never too happy to see him. I can understand the feeling; Kitty for years played second fiddle to Korky; then for some time—after Korky's death—he was King of the Jungle. But now Maxie has arrived. Surely Kitty feels the sting, he can't fail to sense how adorable we judge Maxie to be.

He not only senses, but sees. For on the nights that I can coax Maxie inside, Maxie gets carried in, while Big Kitty gets closed out. Not that Kitty would ever agree to sleep inside; he's a wild outdoor cat, he requires his freedom. But he's peeved.

～

Becky is visiting me when I decide I will carry Maxie inside for his flea powder treatment. My daughter and I stand out on the patio and ring the bell for Maxie. While we wait for his arrival, Becky bends to examine and admire my tall, growing sunflower, a single stalk in a pottery bowl, whose bud is just getting ready to open. Kitty eyes us exclaiming over the flower-to-be.

When Maxie arrives, his little bell jingling, his eyes bright, I swoop him up in my arms and Becky and I go with him into the house, closing the screen behind us.

In a split second, out of the corner of my eye, I see Kitty make a calculated and uncharacteristically fast movement. In no time at all he has leaped into the pottery bowl where the sunflower grows and is squatting into position to use it as a litter box.

"Hey!" I cry, zipping open the screen door and shooing him away. "Hey—what are you doing?"

Becky is laughing behind me.

"You hurt his feelings, Mom!" she says. "He's being naughty."

"He should be happy to have Maxie for company," I say. "He should be happy to have a little brother."

"Do you think I was happy to have a little sister? Not only one, but two?" Becky asks.

"Weren't you?" I say. "I always thought you were delighted!"

June 10

My stop at the thrift shop (also my stalling tactic) on the way to visit my mother turns up the kind of treasures I forget as soon as I get home with them. This time: a plastic caddie for pens and paper clips, a scoop-neck pink cotton sweater (I already have several just like it, which is probably why I buy it), and a framed print of a strange, surreal tree with a burden of hearts—hearts growing on a heart tree like corks grew on the cork tree in a childhood book of mine about Ferdinand the Bull.

I always look on the nightgown rack for a possible new duster or robe for my mother; there is one today, but it has the name of another woman on the collar, in black marker pen. I assume the woman died in a nursing home, and all her clothing was given to the thrift shop. Never mind. I pass on it. Last weekend J. was cleaning out some shelves in the garage and handed me a big lawn bag filled with clothes. They were from my mother's real life: a short blue pleated skirt, a tailored blouse, a gray sweater with blue trim on the collar and cuffs. Still pinned to it was the Tiffany roadrunner pin my mother had always loved (my father had given it to her): a little gold painted bird. I gathered the creature to my face as if it would sing to me. Then I unpinned it from the sweater and handed J. the bag of clothes. "Throw these away if you want to. She's done for. She'll never wear anything again. She'll never come out of there, what do I need them for?" I was thinking of another bag I had in the top of my closet, a bag of my father's clothes, two unwashed shirts, his pajamas—things I rolled up after his death and put away twenty-eight years ago! I wanted to keep his smell. Now I was afraid to discover what odor remained. Mold, I feared. Musty, dusty mold. I didn't need to add my mother's sweet perfume to the mix; I could smell her Estee Lauder "Youth Dew" in my dreams.

On my way out of the thrift shop I see propped against the wall a giant travel poster, mounted on cardboard. "Germany" it declares, and shows a country scene, a snow-tipped mountain in the background, a delicate, thin-spired church, a running stream, a wooden bridge arching across it. A great old tree with sweeping branches is in the foreground. I must have it. I pay my dollar and struggle with the poster to the car, angle and twist it to get it in the back seat, ride with it triumphantly to the nursing home.

I carry the poster in two hands along the street; it's almost as tall as I am, and much wider. A wild wind has come up and tips me like a sail, I dip and spin, it seems to be steering me. I give myself up to the forces of nature, beginning to laugh, moving blindly, the church in the woods preceding me into the double-wide glass doors, held open by a young Mexican aide just about to push through a wheelchair, his charge a tiny bird-like woman.

~

This time I ignore the red warning sign posted on the door frame and enter ungowned, ungloved, unmasked. I will take the risk; my mother has risked far more than this for me, breathed my breath and soothed my body through measles and chicken pox, exposed herself to every contagious childhood disease, swabbed my trench-mouth infected gums with gentian violet, bandaged my bloody knees. I owe her my face and hands, undisguised.

She is asleep with her mouth hanging open. I don't want to see her in this naked unawareness, it's too personal, and too awful. She has made it plain to me that when she dies her casket must be closed, that no one must see her dead. I can understand how that exposure threatens her, how just the thought humiliates her, allows her to imagine the greatest loss of dignity possible. No matter how fancy the casket, how elegantly made-up the face, the hair, how carefully chosen the clothing, how elaborate the funeral, the dead have no advantage at all. No one admiring a mortician's handiwork can voice appreciation with any sincerity, for who wishes to be in that place? Anyone seeing my mother dead is already a trillion times luckier and better off by being—simply—alive. My mother doesn't like to be second best, ever.

"Ma," I say. Awareness dawns slowly, but she comes back to me, her mouth smiles, her eyes fasten on me.

"I've been wanting to tell you," she says without preamble, "one of the young men came in here and said, 'I need five pots.'"

"Five pots?" I say.

"I think he meant 'five bucks' but his English is so bad. I told him I don't have any money, how could I have any money? Maybe he wants a tip. Some other residents have money, they get their hair done, they buy cigarettes. Me, I just lie here like a dog."

"So look what I brought you," I tell her. I stand the poster at the foot of her bed. "It's a travel picture, Mom. What I want you to do, instead of staring at the blank wall, is look at this . . . and do some mind-travel. I want you to wander through these woods, to walk across this bridge and look at the water running over the little stones. I want you to breathe the fresh air, look up at the mountains. I want you to go into the little church and play music on the organ."

"All my organs are no good," she says. She is a genius at getting back to where she wants to be. But I see her eyes examining the poster, which I prop opposite her bed on a little low chest of drawers. I can tell she'll go walking in those woods. I can tell she'll have something to say about it by the next visit.

We go over everything again. How long she's been here, how much she doesn't remember, how she fears she'll have to "be here the rest of my life." This no longer seems like a long time to me, though to her the words carry the idea from her ordinary life. I repeat what I always repeat; why she's here, what happened to her that brought her here, what my phone number is, my birthday, my anniversary, all the addresses at which we used to live.

"How's Maxie?" she asks.

"He's wonderful."

"Is he Maximilian?"

"Yes, you gave him his name. Do you remember? You said he was Maxie, my million."

"I like that name."

"He's so cute, Mom. I notice now that when he eats, he makes little ecstatic sounds, as if he can't believe his good fortune, to get a bowlful of liver/chicken entree, or mariners' feast. It's like the sound I saw a tiger make on some nature program as he was tearing the meat off an animal he killed. It's the sound of the total enjoyment of eating."

"I have no interest in food," my mother says. "None at all. I get all my food through this tube."

No matter where we travel, we come back to the starting point. I wind up our visit. I tell her Maxie is sleeping in the house, and I need to get back to him (which is true).

As I leave the nursing home, I see a display of goods set up in a hallway: T-shirts and wrist watches and blenders and earrings and sets of pots.

"What's going on?" I ask one of the nurses.

"Oh," she says, "they do this every payday. The workers bring in things to sell."

I wonder about this as I walk to my car. Things to sell? It looks like Christmas out in that hallway. Who owns these goods and where were they gotten?

It occurs to me that maybe the aide who asked my mother for "five pots" meant he needed five bucks to buy a pot. Maybe, it occurs to me, I should buy a pot. After all, I didn't do all that well in the thrift shop today. But no, I chide myself. How much do I really need in the way of rewards? I'm alive, aren't I? Isn't that reward enough?

June 12

I can't break Maxie of his habit of nipping delicately at my ankles when it's time to be fed. When at first he would eat anything (cucumber slices, fried onions), now he will eat only from cans labeled "Captain's Feast" and "Mariners' Grill." In a matter of days, his legs seem to have taken on two inches of length, and a solid heft in his midsection makes it harder for me to swoop him up in one arm. Still, his face is kitten-like, tiny and delicate, his tiny triangular skull fits in my palm like a jewel.

The days have turned hot, with afternoon temperatures over a hundred. Today I glance up toward the roof as I am bringing in the mail, and see Maxie hiding under an overhang of shingles, his nose slanted at a dangerous angle toward where I stand on the ground. He must see the question in my face (*How will you get down?*) because he immediately meows helplessly, and drops the question back in my lap.

"Figure it out, Maxie," I say, not unkindly, and while he is doing so, I go inside to get my camera. These moments are like a baby's first steps; they must be recorded—not only in memory but in fact.

First he peers down and takes a reading from several positions on the roof; I walk around to the side of the house where there's a tree (a subtle hint to him), and he considers this tree—assesses its height, its angle, its profusion of branches, and possibly pits them against his limited expertise. (He has climbed up and down trees before; it seems, however, that he forgets he can do it.) He does what my father used to call the old Step 'n' Fetchit dance, three steps forward, two steps back.

Do I have patience for this? We are entertaining tonight; J. has offered our home for the end-of-year department party (at which retirees—and there are four this year—are celebrated). I have a lot of cleaning up to do, much getting ready. Yet Maxie takes his good time, starts down, reconsiders, goes back to a high place on the roof and lies down to rest, comes back, meows, looks at me with his pitiful eyes. I pretend to be studying my wrist watch, and then I hear the rustle of action, his tentative steps onto a branch of the rubber tree (or is it the avocado tree or the mock orange tree—their branches are all intertwined up there), and then there's the sound of claw on bark, the real-business sound of a living body dealing with gravity, the slip and slide of an out-of-control force—too fast, too fast he's coming down. He skids to a halt midway and looks at me.

"Come on," I say. "You can do it." He does it. Fast and no-holds-barred, he tumbles and jumps and lands upright. He looks at me, proud.

"Good boy," I say. "You're wonderful."

~

There are sixty people at the party, many of whom I do not know, nor do they know me. In fact, people pour into my house not really knowing whose house, exactly, it is, and before long, these agreeable strangers (all of them bearing potluck contributions to the gathering) are trying to figure out how to work the microwave, the oven, the various buttons and levers on my kitchen machines. After the first hour of service, warming pans of enchiladas, heating up the chicken casserole, finding a serving utensil for the cactus salad, making coffee (caf and decaf), clanking ice out of the ice maker, distributing paper plates and cups to the right areas, setting out trivets and knives and coasters and every manner of chip and dip, I take myself, exhausted, for a brief respite into the backyard.

Out by the children's old swing set at the far end of the yard, Maxie and Big Kitty are keeping vigil, their faces serious, their expressions suspicious at this invasion, their brows furrowed. Who are these strangers and how long will they stay? (And well they might ask.)

It's a jolly crowd—retirement is always an occasion for back-slapping and jokes and sexual innuendo, punctuated by a few odd and unusual gifts and much laughter. A twenty-pound fudge cake, complete with graceful sugar engraving, has been brought in and placed on the kitchen counter, meant to be presented after the buffet dinner, after the celebratory ceremonies . . . but somehow everyone forgets about this while eating all the other desserts: the chocolate trifle, the pies (meringue, sweet potato, kiwi, blackberry), the caramel popcorn, the cream cheese brownies.

Later, as the guests are filing out, the omission is discovered. "Don't worry," I am assured. "You won't have to eat it all." It's arranged that J. will bring the cake to school on Monday, and the department members will set to it once they've had a day to recover from this horn of plenty.

We are left with other surpluses, the contents of some bowls unrecognizable, but fragrant with chilies, salsa, spices, and very colorful. A large honey-baked ham bone languishes on the table, and when the last guest has gone, I set upon it to salvage shreds for the cats.

I heap these bits of meat upon two flowered paper plates (not previously used) and take them outside so that the cats may share in the bounty of this party. At first they remain invisible—not trusting, I suppose, that it's safe to come back to the house.

But as J. and I sit outside in the cool night air, looking at the misty moon, breathing deeply, the cats of our house creep forth and arrive at our feet to accept their gift of party leftovers.

June 15

A hundred degrees is expected again this afternoon; at 11:00 a.m. I begin a debate with myself. Although I have not visited my mother for five days (the longest I have ever gone without a visit), I feel, somehow, that by now perhaps I have simply visited enough. Maybe enough *is* enough. Maybe I have fulfilled my contract, paid off my obligation, said all that can be said, listened to all that can be heard. Maybe I am done. I don't see why I have to wake up every day and say to myself (even though I have just done this the day before): "Today I must visit my mother."

What has precipitated this feeling I can't exactly say; it may have something to do with the fact that I have been sick myself with a breast infection, that I have visited two doctors myself this week, been probed and pressed, been started on antibiotics that severely upset my stomach, and yesterday—at the surgeon's office—had two needle aspirations of breast cysts, one of which was so painful that I screamed out loud and found myself crying for a long while afterwards. The surgeon himself was mournful, having lost his wife to a terrible disease only twenty-five days before. He said to me, "I know we all must die, but my life is in terrible disarray. I know I will never be the same again."

How this affects my feeling about visiting my mother I do not know, but I feel it has some bearing. Even doctors must face death. There really is no one who escapes. This saddens me in some desperate way.

In any case, I go out, get into the car, drive, because although I feel as if I would like to stay home, stay in bed, go to sleep, wait till I feel better, my other feeling is stronger: I have no choice. She is there, I am here, the two of us must meet and meet again and meet forever till we can no longer meet. I know all too well that the day will come when I will want to see her and she will not be there. That is the undeniable truth. Therefore: I will go today while I have today. While she has today.

~

A familiar figure stands leaning against a familiar car in front of the nursing home. I am slow to perceive that this girl (this *little* girl is really how I see her) who is observing me coming along is my sister; she is here to visit the same woman. The one who is my mother is also her mother. There is no one else to whom this mother is *the* mother.

I am not quite together in my mind; my breast infection may have entered my brain. In England there is a disease called Mad Cow Disease; perhaps I have contracted Mad Cat Disease. Or Mad Max Disease. I even asked the surgeon about this: *Could my new kitten have given me this infection?* The doctor asked me if the cat had scratched my breast. I doubted it, but then, how could I be sure? I often hold Maxie close, he sleeps upon my chest. And then there is his habit of nipping my ankles. Germs, I know, can travel.

The point, however, is clear: I am human, I have a body. I can be sick, too. And how can anyone slightly ill tell her mother how bad she herself feels if her mother is paralyzed, unable to walk, is on a feeding tube and a catheter, and will never enjoy anything again?

My sister and I greet each other with a hug and complain that if two of us visit on the same day, who is going to go the next day?

We walk down the hall of my mother's wing of the nursing home. As we pass the lounge, we hear a cry: "I wish I were dead. I wish I were dead." Looking in the doorway, we see my mother, alone in the room, in her wheelchair, her back toward us, her head in her hand, crying: "I wish I were dead. I wish I were dead."

The sound of the words pierces my heart. She is not doing this for effect, for sympathy, for pity, for entertainment. No one is present. She is saying it because it's true. My sister and I look at each other with fear and clasp each other's hands.

∽

"Mama," I say. I never call her *Mama*. I don't know where that came from, some deep secret place, the place where all children say "Mommy," or "Momma," or "Mama."

She looks up, called back to the world of form and manners: this mother has her children visiting her (both together!) and there is protocol for this.

"I'm so glad to see you," she says. She has truly brightened; she has put away her private pains and private opinions, unwilling to express them for us at this moment. She searches for news to share with us, but what news can there be here?

"I'm on Pampers," she says. "I wear diapers now," she explains. "If I have to go, I do, and I have relief. On that catheter, I never knew if I was going or not."

"But diapers, Ma," I say. (I'm thinking: *My mother in diapers. Is there no end to this?*) "Wouldn't you rather use a bedpan? Call for the nurse?"

"There's no use," she says simply. "They never come in time, and then the whole bed gets wet. This is cleaner. Then the nurses don't have to change the whole bed."

I think how each day she capitulates and capitulates and capitulates. She seems to have gone over to their side, the enemy's side, willing to make it easier for them.

I wait for her to take the usual step back and ask us to see the whole picture, ask us to see how hopeless this is, how impossible the situation, to agree with her vision of the horror of it all—but instead she says, "Yes, I like the diapers better than the catheter, which felt like pins, or knives, in me."

I realize she's doing this for us, making it seem, for our sake, as if life (even this life, in these circumstances) is bearable. This is what all mothers must do for their children, I realize. I do it for mine.

"They're going to weigh me," she announces, when she sees a nurse arrive. "Come along."

We follow behind the nurse who is pushing the wheelchair with one hand, dragging the feeding tube machinery on wheels with her other.

"What's your name?" I ask the nurse.

"Maria."

"They're all Maria here," my mother says, and the nurse laughs. I think how so many of the nurses were named to honor the mother of their god. I think how blessed they must feel, going through life with that kind of protection.

The nurse wheels my mother in her wheelchair up on a little ramp, and takes a digital reading of the weight that registers on the dial. Then (although it's the same wheelchair she's always in and must weigh the same every time) they call for an aide to lift my mother out of the wheelchair. A young woman (also Maria?) lifts my mother up almost to a standing position. My mother cries out, "Oh! Oh! Oh!" and quickly a reading of the weight of the wheel chair is taken. My mother is replaced. "Oh get me back to bed," she says. "Can you? Can you? I can't be up anymore." Then she turns to the nurse. "What do I weigh?"

"One hundred twenty-two pounds."

"Really?" my mother says proudly. "I never weighed that much in all my life. I never weighed more than 108."

"You must be eating well," says one of the Marias. "You must like the food here."

And I look at the feeding machine: the arrow that turns, the motor that hums, the tube that feeds sixty-five cubic centimeters of carefully measured nutritionally balanced chalky beige fluid into the hole in my mother's belly each hour.

My mother smiles at the joke. No fuss, no mess, no shopping, no cooking, no dishes to clean up, no chewing, no swallowing. My mother has always been a *prima donna*. Maybe, in some weird, sad, amazing way, she is finally being waited on hand and foot, she is finally the princess she always wanted to be.

June 18

A call from a nurse at the nursing home informs me that "your mother asked me to call you and tell you she misses you."

Well, yes, Mother, I say to myself. *I last saw you two days ago, this is the third day on which I have let the sun rise and the moon set and have not been at your side. I have been thinking of other things, living my other life. I, too, Mother, have business with doctors, have had to see my doctor again, suffer the consequences of time passing, feel fear at the malfunction of something or other in this body of mine that you made, Mother.*

I wonder what started me off on this track, put me in this miserable state of mind.

But she has never before *asked* me or my sister to come, never before so much as tilted the guilt lever. Even as I argue with myself (as usual) that I don't have to visit so often, I get ready to go; I finish sealing the bills on my desk and stamping them, I load the dishes in the dishwasher, take the damp towel out from under it to dry on the pool wall, bring in the empty cat dishes and rinse them.

(I realize with fury at this exact moment that the blasted dishwashing machine still leaks intermittently. J. has never fixed it or allowed that it needs to be fixed, and I have never made my stand. That's it! I decide. Enough is enough. Today I will call the plumber and my husband can divorce me if he likes!)

I recognize I must be reaching the end of my rope. I make sure there is water outside for Maxie and Big Kitty, I gather up the bills to be mailed, I take with me the publisher's catalog that announces my new book of stories (so my mother can be proud), I take some snapshots I've had developed of the party that was held in our house (she often says she can't remember my house, can't picture it at all), I look around and think what else I can bring to that tiny cell of a room—maybe a flower for her to smell, maybe a peppermint candy.

I have offered to bring her "talking books" that she could listen to on a cassette player (she says she has no interest in listening to anything); I have brought her a table radio she has shunned, a Walkman (with earphones) that she has refused. I have suggested large print books (no), a larger TV with remote control (no), a small electronic keyboard on which she might pick out tunes with her good hand (no, it would break her heart now that she can't play with both hands).

So I go: with myself only, mainly, me, her daughter, whom she misses.

$\sim$

And there, again, by coincidence, or fate, or karma, or destiny, is her other daughter, my sister, who has turned up at the same moment I have. Maybe we are recognizing the countdown: be here today, there may be no tomorrow.

Elena is there at her side, the wide-bodied, sweet-hearted Mexican aide, and she is clipping my mother's nails. My mother is in good humor; it's almost like a party, with my sister there, and me there, and Elena with her long dark ponytail and her colorful emery boards and silver nail clippers.

"You have such good children," she tells my mother, and yes, my mother agrees, she is proud.

"My wonderful girls," she says. "One is a writer. One is an artist." (She used to say of the three of us, including herself, "Here we are, the musician, the artist, and the writer.")

My sister demurs, she has given up that conceit some time ago. "I like to draw," she says. "But just a little."

"Well, I have something to show you," I say, handing my mother the publisher's catalog which shows the cover of my new book: it has on it a large, impressionistic heart, almost a valentine heart, but shimmery, its outlines vague and imperfect, its pink and gray colors bleeding onto the page.

My mother reads the book description and then pronounces aloud the words that describe me: ". . . prize winning, acclaimed, among her many honors . . . ."

"You're an important person," she says.

"Well"—I let this stand, it's important to her that I be important—"if I am, you made me so."

"You've done good things in the world," she says.

"Yes, and I hope my children will do good things." I nod in my sister's direction, ". . . and my sister's children will do good, too, and their children will do good . . . and, think of it, Mom, all this good begins with you." I begin to suspect this may sound like a eulogy, and I stop carrying on, but my mother has got into the mood of this.

"It's all like a big heart," she suggests, indicating the book-jacket heart at which we have just been looking. "Heart after heart, on and on in time."

"On and on in time," I repeat.

Tears flood my mother's eyes, perhaps at the thought of this endless cycle of love and good things and hearts.

My sister gets up from the chair and throws her purse over her shoulder. "Well, let's not get too emotional here, I don't want to have a major breakdown," she says. "I have shopping to do." She laughs. "I'd better go."

"You go, too," my mother says to me. "My wonderful girls." She observes us with pride. "No one ever had better children," she tells Elena.

"Don't get carried away, Mom," my sister says. "We're not exactly angels."

"You're *my* angels."

"Little angels from heaven," Elena adds.

My sister and I tell my mother we love her, we throw her kisses, we throw Elena kisses, and we walk out to the parking lot. Suddenly, standing between our cars, we both, at the same moment, begin to flap our arms. Like angels, we are growing wings. We don't seem to get off the ground, however, flapping around like a couple of old chickens. This brings on one of our famous, hysterical laughing fits as we stumble about, falling into one another's arms. Through our wrenching laughter, through our wild, helpless tears, my sister tries to talk. She wants to know: how many angels can crack up on the head of a pin?

July 12

A long hiatus: there is no news, the summer moves along. Maxie is maintaining, my mother is maintaining. Each one gains weight, my mother's feeding tube spinning its arrow of bland vitamin-packed beige fluid into her stomach night and day, while Maxie learns to gulp and gobble his kibble, his raw egg, his ground fish innards. Each one lives on his own terms, concentrates on life, on keeping it, according to his needs and situation. As my mother grows heavier, planted deep in her bed like a boulder in a valley, Maxie defies gravity, runs faster over the earth, climbs higher in the trees, seems at times to fly.

I have been busy with work, with visitors, with obligations. I teach at a writers' conference, I cook splendid meals for my daughter Joanna and the friend she has brought home with her for two weeks, I attend the unveiling of my uncle's gravestone and console my aunt, my mother's sister, when she examines the empty space next to my uncle's grave.

When I visit my mother and tell her about the unveiling, she inquires, sharp-eyed, about *her* space in that cemetery—is it still empty, is it to my father's right or left, is her gravestone laid yet? "I can't wait to join him," she tells me.

"There's no hurry," I say. "Eternity is long, Ma."

My mother's new roommate, a delicate, birdlike woman named Ruby who has a hip infection, who is in isolation with my mother because they share a common germ, says to me, "I haven't had my dust yet today. When do you suppose they will bring my dust?"

"She's always hungry!" my mother says angrily. "She doesn't remember from one minute to the next that she's eaten." She rolls her eyes. "That woman's mind is gone, it's gone," my mother says. "If I have to live with her another minute, I'll kill myself."

One way or another, it seems my mother is determined to get into that empty grave. I know that gravesite too well. It's on a hillside, a steep incline that slants down toward the freeway. For days after my father died, twenty-eight years ago, it rained. My mother, staying at our house with us, stared out the window at the downpour and said, "Can his coffin slide down the hill? Can he tumble to one end of it and be stuck there, all bunched up? Will he get wet? Will he float away?" My sister and I had chosen the site only days before, as my father lay dying. We had discussed, most seriously, the beauty of the view, the noise level of passing cars, the added benefit of the nearby freeway, from which we could wave at him whenever we passed by in years to come. We even decided our father would appreciate the bridle path, the sound of the horses' hooves on hard sand, the voices of the young men and women riding together. And then we laughed. I remember how we looked at each other and burst out in our particular brand of wild, hysterical laughter, how our eyes teared, how we choked and clung to each other.

Now I say the comforting, dismissive things to my mother: that Ruby is mostly quiet, she has no loud TV, she's especially genteel, she was once a person of some education, some intelligence. To prove it I ask her, "Were you ever a school teacher, Ruby?"

"I was a secretary."

"Were you a good typist?"

"I was the best. But of course, that was when . . . that was in my other life."

I am silent. For everyone here, in this nursing home, there is this life, such as it is, and there is the other life—the one that's over.

I can't help but imagine myself someday living in half a room, far from anyone who loves me. Without my permission or knowledge, some stranger has been brought in to live in the other half, someone I don't know, haven't met, someone I will have to hear breathing in the night, whose bodily ills I am forced to be intimately acquainted with, whose cries of pain I will have to hear, whose visitors' chatter I will be required to witness.

Impossible! I think. *Intolerable!* What about my space? My privacy? My right to be with those who know me? Who *love* me?

But I sing Ruby's praises to my mother; it could be worse is what I'm really saying. It has been worse. My mother has been in a room with a dead woman. She has been in a room with a moaning, permanently comatose woman. She has shared her space with babblers and screamers, religious fanatics and stroke victims, with those who watched baseball or westerns or preachers on TV. Luckily my mother can't remember most of these partners. I remember all of them. I am my mother's memory.

~

Maxie, somehow, has lost his little bell. He comes to me silently, over the grass, hopping more like a gazelle now than a bunny. His long hind legs are graceful, he bounds in connected arcs, almost in slow motion. He still comes for greeting, for company, for love—never just for food. He can wait for food; he trusts it will be forthcoming, he never makes me feel as if I am only the purveyor of his "mariners' delight."

His gaze is as intense as ever, his soft paw-pads walking up my chest, to stroke my throat, are still just as touching to me, but he has a quality of knowing-it-all now, a blasé aspect. He no longer is astonished by a bird, a butterfly, a bug. He can hear a dog bark without so much as cocking his ears. He knows the dogs who live next door, he knows they are behind a tall fence, he doesn't bother to be fearful.

A spider web on the wall no longer sends him into a frenzy of exploration, nor does a sprinkle of catnip fling him into ecstasy. He, like the rest of us, finds that life is not all manic discovery; even a kitten hasn't the energy to stay at that level of adventure, of passion. Maxie sleeps more; he comes to my bell ringing, or to my call, more slowly, more certain of what he will find. He's growing up. He's slowing down. He's pacing himself for the long haul ahead.

July 17

Leroy, the aide who does TV repair as a side job, has replaced the antenna on my mother's TV set, but he has refused to tell her what we "owe" him.

"He says he doesn't want to trouble me," my mother says, "but that he'll wait to speak to you. So see if you can find him." Just then, Leroy passes by in the hall and stops at the door of my mother's room. He waves to us. He's a black man with dark, dark skin and a beautiful warm smile.

"Oh, please, Leroy," I say. "Can you come in for a minute—I want to give you what we owe you."

"I'll be back in five minutes," he says. He disappears.

My mother says to me, "What if he overcharges you?"

"How much could he charge, Mom? The whole little TV is only worth fifty dollars."

"He could take advantage," my mother says. "You know how the world is."

"Let's not worry," I say. "He takes very good care of you, he's a very good man. So please don't discuss it, I want to pay him whatever he asks."

"What if he asks a hundred dollars? Will you pay that much?"

I sigh. I get so out of breath when I visit my mother. I have to talk and talk, argue and argue, explain and explain.

Now her roommate, Ruby, in the other bed, says to me, sweetly,

"Have you come to help me escape? Do you have some money to give me? I'd like you to call a cab right now. The only thing is, I can't think of a place in the world where I can go."

"This goes on all day," my mother says. "I wish I could die right now. I can't take any more of this. She talks all the time, she says she weighs five hundred pounds, she's out of her mind."

"Shh," I whisper to my mother. Ruby is not four feet away. I never understand how my mother can talk about others as if they don't exist.

"Have they sent you for me?" Ruby asks. "I've been waiting for days and days. I've never been in a mess like this before. I must get out of here."

"You want to get out of here and my mother wants to get out of here," I say to Ruby. "I really do understand how you both feel. You feel trapped in your poor, tired bodies."

"Oh yes," Ruby says gratefully. "Yes, that's true. I'm so glad you know what it's like." She has the face of a ballet dancer—narrow, pointed, delicate; her white hair is tied back with a ribbon. It's clear she was once (this is the thing they say about old women) a great beauty.

"She's crazy," my mother says.

"I wish both of you could fly out of here," I tell them. "I wish you both had wings and could just leave together, go right over the rooftops, go on to some fine adventure together."

"I'd go home," Ruby says, "if I had a home."

"I have no home," my mother says. "What could I call my home now?"

"Your mind is your home, Ma," I say. "All the things you remember."

"I remember nothing. My memory is gone. I wish I were dead."

"I wonder if you remember Allen Berk," I say. "He used to live next door to us in Brooklyn. His mother and you talked to each other through your kitchen windows. I used to play Monopoly with him."

"I don't remember him. I don't remember anything."

"He was killed just the other day, Ma."

"Who?"

"Allen Berk. The little boy who lived next door to us. He became a famous lawyer. About two weeks ago some crazy man walked into his law firm in San Francisco and killed eight people. He was one of them."

I hadn't meant to tell this to my mother, but it seems the right time to jar her into some memory of her long life.

"His mother was a screamer. She was always yelling at him," she says. "It's a wonder he didn't shoot *her.*"

"So you do remember him and his family?"

"Who could forget them?" she says.

"When I saw his name in the paper, I was shocked."

Ruby seems to be listening to us. But what she says is, "They didn't bring my sand today, either. My sister should be here soon. My husband worked in the produce markets, he bought lettuce."

"Oh, she has no husband," my mother says. "She's crazy. I wish they would bring my milk of magnesia. I asked for it hours ago."

"I see the nurse in the hall. Maybe she's bringing it now."

"Close my window curtains," my mother says. "Whoever the madman was who killed Allen Berk might decide to shoot me."

"The man is dead," I say. "He killed himself when the police cornered him in a stairwell."

"Then some other nut could be loose, trying to get me."

The charge nurse comes in, gowned, gloved, and masked. I tend to forget I'm supposed to put on all these items; the red sign is still on the door although I don't believe my mother really has any contagious condition.

"Medicine, Jessie," the nurse says. She proceeds to mix some pink fluid in a plastic cup and draws it into a transparent syringe. She uncaps my mother's feeding tube and injects the fluid into the plastic tube.

"Oh, I'm getting wet," my mother cries. "Oh, I feel it all the way up in my chest. Now it's coming up into my throat, my mouth. I hate it."

"Just your medicine, Jessie," the nurse says calmly. She wipes up the spill with a towel and pats my mother's leg. "Night, Jessie."

"Who's going to change my diaper?"

"Soon Leroy will be in," the nurse says. She leaves the room without formal goodbyes. I want to leave, too. I want to leave as badly as Ruby and my mother want to leave. Maybe the three of us can link angel-wings and fly away over the rooftops.

Leroy comes in, his black skin in vivid contrast against his white uniform. He says to Ruby, "How's my most beautiful lady in the world feeling tonight?"

"Oh, Leroy," I cry. "What about my mother? Isn't she beautiful?"

"Ah yes," he says. "She, too, is my most beautiful."

Both old women are smiling. I can't believe it. They have beautiful, wonderful smiles on their toothless mouths.

"So, Leroy," I say. "Let's settle up for the work you did on Mother's television."

He looks heavenward, as if he is counting. For a moment, being my mother's daughter, I imagine he will say, "That will be two hundred dollars."

"It was nothing," he says. "Hardly anything at all. Don't worry about it."

"Tell me what to pay you. Please."

"The part cost five dollars. That's all."

I take a twenty-dollar bill out of my purse and hand it to him.

"Oh no," Leroy says. "Nothing like that."

"We all appreciate how kind you are to my mother," I tell him, not knowing if that is the wrong thing to say. "This isn't exactly like winning the lottery."

"To me it is," he says. "I never expected this much."

"Take it, please."

Shyly, Leroy places it in his shirt pocket.

Ruby asks urgently if he has brought her sand. My mother asks for her milk of magnesia, forgetting the nurse has just been in with it. She tells Leroy she wants her diaper changed.

Her diaper. I feel dizzy with exhaustion. "Ma," I say. "My back hurts. I want to go home and lie down."

Ruby says to me, "You are such a darling girl. Did you come here to take me away?"

"No, Ruby, I came to visit my mother."

"Who *are* you visiting?" my mother accuses me. "Me or her?"

"Ruby, I can't talk to you anymore just now. I have to talk to my mother. Why don't you rest and be quiet for a little while?"

"Oh, that's a good idea," she says. "That's really what I want. I've had ten heart attacks, you know."

"She's crazy," my mother says. "I want you to see if you can get my room changed."

"Do you really want me to? Ruby is very pleasant, Mom."

"I'm going mad."

"Okay, I'll speak to the administrator in the morning."

"But who knows what I'll get, then? I could get someone who plays the TV day and night. At least this one is soft-spoken."

Oh God, I think. Get me out of here. Leroy has gone out to the hall and comes back in carrying a large blue diaper. I know I don't want to see this man diaper my mother.

"Ma, I have to go home."

"I hope I have a big heart attack in my sleep and don't live to get up tomorrow."

"Fine," I say, "but I can't talk about it now. I'm going home. I hope you will be alive tomorrow. I can't wish for you to die."

"But you should," she says. "You know it's the only way I can get out of this."

"It will happen soon enough."

"Sand," Ruby says. "I need sand and sand and sand."

"Ma, turn on your TV," I say. "Watch the world go by."

"You should go home, darling," she says, suddenly. "Go home and rest. I love you. Thank you for coming."

"Goodnight," Ruby says.

"She has no children," my mother says. "She thinks she does, but she doesn't. It's a pity."

Leroy, the one who is an angel, pulls back my mother's covers. She willingly submits to his ministrations.

"Good-bye," I call over my shoulder. I flee down the hall, running, stopping only at the rest room to wash my hands and face with cool water. I use a paper towel to open the door and hold it in my hand to open the front door of the nursing home. I carry it all the way out to the car. My thought is that I don't want to contaminate my steering wheel with the violence of old age.

~

In the thrift shop I buy a box of greeting cards—a shoe box full of them for a mere $1.50. What a buy! What a bargain! When I get home I exultantly examine my treasure. These days, when one card costs $1.50, I have walked off with a jackpot of perhaps fifty of them.

I begin to thumb through the cards, thinking about which ones might be suitable for what occasions. There's one that says, "Thinking of You," and inside shows a grubby man with a stubbly beard staring at a bottle of Drano. Another, a birthday card, says, "May you live to be a hundred and be shot in bed by a jealous husband." Another suggests, "Let's Do It In The Road."

Well, maybe these aren't such a bargain after all.

But then I see one card that causes me to catch my breath; it's not a greeting card but a note card. The painting on it invites my heart rhythm to change. What I see is a scene at the edge of a river; it may be sunset or sunrise, but a glowing path of light angles across the river to the bank where three hooded souls stand bidding farewell to the fourth, a being who is shown setting out from shore in a small canoe. She is facing away from the others (I am sure, at once, it is a "she") and is beginning a journey in the frail vessel that drifts away from shore toward the great beam of light. Her fingers clutch the sides of the boat tightly, in the way that a child hangs on to a ride that she fears but also anticipates greatly. The lone voyager has no provisions with her, no oars, no compass, no maps—she's clearly on her own, floating on the illuminated water toward some destination she does not know.

I am overcome by emotion as I look at this picture. It is my mother in the boat, and I am one of the three hooded supplicants bidding her farewell. We, on the shore, have our hands upturned; we are not trying to keep her with us, or stop her, or shout encouragement to her—we simply stand and watch, there to witness her leaving, to bid her farewell, to see her dwindle toward the light.

I turn the card over and see that the painting's title is "The Blessing" and the artist is Nancy Bright. Is this a religious painting? Surely it's full of mystery and beauty and peace. I don't know why I am so sure the person sailing away is my mother, but I am certain it's her form under the robe and hood, those are her hands hanging on tight, helping her to be brave and strong and balanced. And though I can't see her eyes, I know they're staring ahead, at the light, and at the coming mystery.

I stand on shore, physically feeling the slanting riverbank under my feet, watching her go, feeling as I did when I sent my first child off to kindergarten, and the last child off to college.

Goodbye, goodbye. I can't go with you. I can't protect or follow you. I love you and hope for your safe journey. But I wonder—oh I wonder!—if I can I live without you.

July 22

Bureaucracy triumphs as I sleep; an early morning phone call from the nursing home informs me they are going to move my mother to another wing.

"But why?" I cry from the fog of my dreams, trying to will my heartbeat back to a regular cadence. The phone, ringing at seven, has the effect on me of a knife stab. For the nursing home staff it is merely the hour the shift changes; the on-duty, early-morning social worker wants to get her duties under way.

"Your mother's Medicare time is up," she says briskly. "Time to move her."

"But . . ." I stammer and actually hear myself say, "she likes it where she is!"

"Sorry, her time is up," says the woman. "We just have to inform you."

"Do you know where they're putting her?"

"We have several empty beds. No, I don't know exactly. Whatever's available."

I resist in my mother's behalf. A new bed, new roommate, a new view of the clock, the wall, new caretakers. These are radical changes for a person of great age. I think of the intricate, exact life she has had us rig for her; the little TV just so on the table; the page of the calendar I tape for her on the rails of her bed each month; the poster of the bucolic German landscape propped on the dresser opposite her bed, the photo of my daughter Susanna (framed) and the dust jacket of my new book, *This Old Heart of Mine*, propped side-by-side against the base of the German poster, where she can see them.

She depends for dear life on the faces that float into view: Leroy, who makes her smile; Elena, who showers her on Tuesdays and Fridays and transfers her from wheelchair to bed; Hoda, who always says, "Don't be so nervous, Jessie, calm down, Sweetie"; and the charge nurse on each shift, who appears with the mystical potions to inject into her feeding tube. There are the myriad employees who sweep the floor, who stock the paper-towel holder, who change the bulbs. These people have become my mother's family in the last months. Now she will be orphaned, dumped into a new wing, where no one knows her, knows her routine, knows her habits. *Where no one loves her!* (Well, yes, I am putting myself in her place, but how can I not?)

I look at my own bedside table as I talk on the phone: my water glass, *there,* and my eyeglasses, *there,* and my lip balm, *there,* and my cup with pens and emery boards and a little mirror in it; yes, I am compulsive about these things that make up my world, no less than my mother is about the exact position of her TV table, her tissue box, the angle between her eye and the picture of Susanna.

"Do you think someone can tell me which room or rooms they're planning to put her in? I'd like to visit, talk to some of her possible roommates before we move her."

"I don't see why not," says the social worker. "Why don't you call the administrator at nine, when she gets into her office, and talk to her? We won't move your mother right now. We can wait a day or so."

"Oh thank you! Thank you! I'll be in this morning, as soon as I can."

≈

Armed with the numbers of the rooms that have an empty bed, I set out to interview the prospective roommates with whom my mother may have to live. I feel a pang of pity for these faceless souls—I will be intruding upon them in their precious, temporary privacy. I will be smiling, courteous, selling my mother to them: "My mother is completely alert, her mind is fine, she's very bright, she watches *Jeopardy* and *Wheel of Fortune*." *(But she hates soap operas. By the way, do you happen to watch TV all day?)*

There are nine wings in this convalescent hospital—it stretches in all directions like a giant octopus. I begin my quest with a room in the 800 wing (my mother lived there earlier, when she could still walk, still play the piano). As soon as I enter, I realize this room is impossible: a taint of cigarette smoke hangs in the room like a pall. A woman, not-smoking, sits by the window patting her permanented hair into place. She turns a smile upon me—I'm struck by the gleam of even, false teeth. A large gilded crucifix hangs on the wall; a beaded rosary hangs from her bony fingers.

"Oh, I have the wrong room," I tell her, and back out—fast. I make my way past the inhabited wheelchairs in the hall; nodding, saying hello, ignoring the outstretched hands, the pleas for one urgent favor or another ("Take me to my room," "I need the nurse," "Get me a taxi, I have to get out of here"). I look into a room in the 900 wing—here a tall woman is reading a romance novel (and has several others in her lap). At the same time she is watching a soap opera. I tell her the reason for my errand, that my mother will be moving into a new room, maybe even this one.

"I like my privacy," says the woman. "Don't have her come here."

"It isn't my choice . . ." I begin to explain. Then I simply say, "Well, thanks, good-bye."

In the 600 unit, I find the last of the designated rooms, and in it sits an ancient woman facing a wallful of family photographs. I introduce myself, and she says, "What, what? I'm ninety-two, I'm hard of hearing. I'm very tired. They gave me a shower this morning." I explain my mission; I begin to examine the photos on the wall. The woman, whose name is Jenny Rosenstein, must be of the same ethnic background as my mother. I have these same kinds of photos in my photo album at home—relatives from the Old Country: Russia, Poland, Romania.

"I'll take it," I think to myself. This is a room where I could bear to visit. This woman could be my grandmother. But no, my grandmother would be well over a hundred now—I am no spring chicken myself. I tell her about my mother. She isn't furious; she seems even interested. "I don't know what they do here, but if she wants to come in here, it's all right with me."

"Oh thank you! Thank you. Nice to meet you."

"I'm in very bad shape, you know," she tells me. "I fell and broke my hip. I've had a stroke. I can't even hold a few pages of anything in my hand."

"Oh, my mother, too!" I say, full of excitement. "The same thing!"

"I'm no good for anything."

"Neither is she." We both smile. "I'll go tell her I met you."

$\sim$

"I found you a roommate, Ma," I tell my mother, after I explain that she will have to be moved out of the Medicare wing. "She's Jewish. She has the same troubles you do. She does have a TV, but I think she might wear headphones when she watches it—I saw them there."

"When can I go?"

"Are you in a hurry?"

"I don't know what I'm in a hurry for," my mother says bitterly. "Believe me, you don't want to know what I'm in a hurry for."

July 26

I avoid being there for the move; I arrive with J. after it is accomplished and find both old ladies in extreme distress. My mother's new bed is too high, there are no pillows on it, the call bell is situated in such a way that she cannot reach it with her "good" hand, the room is too small, her bed is too close to the window, there is no bathroom in the room, Jenny is so deaf that whenever she talks, she shouts, and because she can't hear, my mother has to shout back to answer her. My mother can't believe she's lost all she had—which now seems incredibly valuable: her bed, her call bell, her pillows, her other roommate.

I don't know where to begin: pillows seem easiest—surely they can find two pillows for her. But no, they can't. The supply room is closed for the day; they have no idea what happened to her other pillows, and besides, those pillows belong to Unit Five and this is Unit Six. But they'll do a pillow-search. And what about the call-button, which is located on my mother's paralyzed side? And what about . . .

J. sees I am breathless with trying. I sit down and let him talk, I catch my breath. Jenny has clamped her earphones on her head and wheeled herself to within one inch of her large television set. She determinedly turns on the TV and applies her eyes to the images on the screen. She wants not to experience what is going on here—it's too disruptive to a woman in her nineties, too threatening. And so, when two men come in, pushing another (lower) bed for my mother, they push Jenny carefully out of the way, and she flails out in panic. She has no idea what's happening, only that two men are pushing her away from her television set (to which she is attached by the earphones and their wires).

"Where are they taking me?" she screams. "Where? Where?"

"It's okay," I scream back to her, patting her arm. "They're just moving in a bed for my mother."

"Oh, why does she have to be here?" Jenny moans. "My life was quiet before."

My mother makes an ugly face. "Do you think I want to be here? Do you think I want to be alive?"

Oh God. J. looks at my face and stands up. "Let them work it out," he says. "Your mother needs time to adjust."

"I wish I were dead!" my mother says.

"I know, Ma. I know. Give this a chance. In a day or two all these things will be taken care of."

"I hope I don't live a day or two," she says.

~

At home, I find Maxie on the doorstep and scoop him up in my arms. I cradle him, croon to him, sit with him in a big chair and kiss his face. He is in the mood for love. He stares into my eyes. He climbs up, up to my face, and nuzzles my neck, nips me gently on the tip of my chin. His teeth are like tiny rough diamonds, they sparkle in the nerves of my skin, but they don't hurt. *Oh Maxie, Maxie,* I say, *Oh Maxie I love you, Oh Maxie I wish there weren't so much sadness in the world, Oh Maxie I wish old age were a happier time, I hope I don't get old, I hope you don't get old, I hope you will love me forever.*

Maxie talks to me, a little chirping sound, a cross between a squawk and a song. He makes it once; it's mysterious cat-speech, it's an answer to all I have said.

He rests his small head against my breast; I feel tears run down my cheek; I see tears fall onto his fur. If only there were no pain in the world. If only we all lived forever.

July 30

Is that my mother? As I come down the breezeway on my way to the 600 Unit, I see—through the open door of the "activity room"—a woman sitting in a wheelchair. She is white-haired (but aren't they all?) and attached to a feeding tube (as are so many), and she has that vacant stare that inhabits the faces of the very old. She is slumped forward with the posture that spells, not patience, but resignation. Still—I'm not sure. Is it she? Could it be someone else, some other woman's mother? I draw closer, staring, and see what's bothering me: this woman has a slash of red across her mouth, lipstick is smeared on her face, without regard for the shape of her lips, in a thick red line.

"Mom?"

She looks up, her eyes clear, turn alert, her face brightens, she comes alive. "I'm so glad to see you."

She is, I can feel it. I kiss the top of her head. I take her hand.

"They brought me in here."

From her tone, I know what I am supposed to see as I look around. Not a crowd of aged angels, waiting patiently for release, for distraction, for some crumb of pleasure, but a roomful of catatonics, half of them with their heads thrown back, their mouths open, their eyes closed—and the rest in various stages of palsy or spasm, drooling, moaning, shouting. The variety of wheelchairs, padded orthopedic chairs, feeding tubes, life-sustaining equipment, makes me think we could be in Lourdes.

"So, Ma," I say. "How are you?" In the background, a tape is playing, some inspirational song about salvation and Jesus. My eye lands on the face of an astonishingly young woman, stretched out in one of the oddly padded reclining chairs. She could be twelve, she could be perhaps twenty-five, but is still eons younger than the other residents. Her arms are as thin and brittle-looking as toothpicks, her eyes are huge, dark, staring seriously at each face as she rotates her head in a small arc from side to side.

"Ma, look at that young woman. Do you know who she is?" The young woman's hair is very short and dark; she can't weigh more than eighty pounds, if that much.

My mother glances, turns away. She isn't interested. She doesn't see what I see, feel the pang I feel to see someone so young living here. She wants my attention. "On the way here, the aide who was wheeling me over stopped and said, 'Just a minute, I want to do something,' and then she came back and smeared lipstick all over my face. I don't even know whose lipstick it was. I don't have one here."

"Why didn't you tell her you don't want lipstick?"

"I didn't know what she was going to do! I didn't have any warning."

"Tomorrow you tell her you don't want makeup," I say. "You must assert yourself."

"It's easy for you to say," my mother tells me. "You have no idea what goes on here. That woman in my room wants to go to sleep at eight o'clock; she wants the curtains open or she wants them closed, she wants the light off or she wants it on, she's crazy, she's completely crazy."

Suddenly the music is shut off and a tall good-looking man with a loud, deep voice begins to talk—as if to a congregation. "Folks, you must be waiting for your miracle. How well I know what you feel. Because every year on my anniversary, I ask myself: 'Is my wife going to come back to me this year?'—and I'm downcast and depressed when she doesn't. But hey—it's just a matter of attitude. This last year on my anniversary, I said something else to myself. I said, 'If she hasn't come back yet, I'm just that much closer to the day when she will!'"

The man laughs and turns up the volume on some kind of jazzy, hand-clapping hymn; when it's over, he says, "So how many are waiting for a miracle? All of you, I think. So what's your attitude going to be? You have to say, 'I'm not on my time-scale, I'm on the time-scale of Jesus, and if it's not today, it's tomorrow.' The best thing you can tell yourself is that you're just that much closer to the day it will happen."

My mother looks at me and widens her eyes; I know what she's thinking. This is not for her. "Ma, you'll have to tell them you don't want to come to this activity; you're not suited for a revival."

"You tell them. Do you think I have the strength to tell them everything?"

∽

I seek out the administrator and explain the problem to her. "I don't wish to offend anyone, but my mother is Jewish; this is not her world." There is some puzzlement in her face—I'm reminded again of how surprised Christians are to be made aware there are people around who do not believe in their doctrines. She says she will look into where else my mother may be taken for the activity hour.

∽

I stop in my mother's room to deliver a small night light that might solve the conflict between her and Jenny. Jenny, sitting in her wheelchair, staring at the wall, smiles to see me, asks me my name (again), and tells me that she's sorry my mother screams, over and over, "I wish I were dead."

"Does it bother you?"

"Of course it bothers me. I'm ninety-two and in pain all the time, but I don't scream. If you live this long, you have to put up with certain things."

"Would you like me to have my mother moved out of your room?"

"She'll just scream somewhere else."

"But you won't have to listen to it."

"Then someone else will. Or I'll get someone else with other troubles." She shrugs. "You can't have anything you want here, you know."

An aide, passing in the hall, sees me and says, "We have no more diapers for your mother."

"Well, can you get some?"

"They only pay for them in the Medi*care* wing, not the Medi*cal* wing."

"I don't understand. What are the Medi*cal* patients supposed to do if they need diapers?"

The aide doesn't know. I want to question the decision to put my mother in diapers in the first place. I know it was done for the convenience of the staff, to reduce the call for the bedpan—which my mother often did not get in time and wet the bed, anyway—but now she has become used to having no control over her bladder at all.

"Medi*cal* can't pay for Pampers; they are very expensive, more than fifty dollars a box," the aide says.

I try to calculate how many boxes my mother would need in a month. More trouble. More things to straighten out. Does it ever end? I feel like those angels in the activity room waiting for a miracle. I have to remember that in the nursing home we're not on People Time; here we are on God's time.

August 3

J. and I go out to buy a light fixture for the bathroom, and innocently I suggest, "Let's stop off and see Mother for a few minutes on our way." Of course he agrees.

This is a day one might characterize as "hot as hell"— though I am not thinking in metaphors as we park in the shade of a leafy tree. I'm wearing a new dress I bought in the thrift shop, sleeveless, scoop-necked, cotton, with a flared swishy skirt and emblazoned with big splashy pink flowers. My step is light—I feel hopeful, pretty, energized (feelings I never question when I've got them). I really want to see my mother today, to see her eyes see me, to please her in some way. So it's a double shock when I enter my mother's room with J. behind me and see her burning red eyes. She's alone in the room, deep in some private fury, thrashing in a pit of anger.

She begins at once: she has a terrible pain in her right side but they turn her to lie on it, nevertheless, in order that she not get bedsores. She can't reach the pull cord and at night can't see (since two cords are knotted together) which one is blue (the light switch) and which one is red (the call cord). She can't reach her little TV since someone has pushed her table out of reach. The July calendar page is still on the wall, so she doesn't even know what month it is. They don't let her use the shower chair often enough for bowel movements. And though she told them she hasn't had a BM for days, some nurse stuck a finger inside her and told her she wasn't impacted—"There's nothing there."

I take a deep breath. The turmoil I feel boiling up within me has to do, oddly, with embarrassment. (Must she speak so openly about her bowels in the presence of my husband? Where is her sense of decorum?) And then I am ashamed; there is no such thing as decorum in moments of mortal extremity. There was no sense of decorum in the cattle cars going to Auschwitz. This woman, my mother, is powerless and has no control over the simplest matter of the sort we all take for granted, like her bowels, or the light switch. She can't turn herself from side to side—aides turn her as if she is a sack of hay. And here I have come flouncing in like a can-can girl, with my twirly skirt, feeling—daring to feel—cheerful, thinking she would actually be happy to see me.

"Ma," I say, going to stand beside her bed rails. "Ma!"—and her face crumples and she begins to cry, cry with all her might: "Oh please—I want to be dead, I want to be dead. I want a coffin in the cemetery, I want to be in a coffin, I just want to sleep, I just want to sleep, please, please, I don't want to be alive!"

This is a new level of desperation she has reached. I begin to stroke her hair back over her forehead, over and over, I press her white hair back and I do it again, harder and faster. Tears are running from my eyes as she cries, "Please, I want to die and I don't know how."

"You will, Ma, you will," I say. "We all die. Life is not infinite. For anyone. It will happen. You're getting there."

"I try and I try but I don't know how to die," she begs me.

I'm speechless. I look at J. He stares at me. I feel as if I can't bear it. I really can't.

My mother sees this is true, and she says, finally, "I shouldn't be doing this to you."

"You're not doing it to me," I say, ". . . life does it to all of us."

I look at J. to help me, but he's speechless, stricken also by her earnest wish, her impossible predicament.

All right, I'll do what I can do, which isn't much. I'll tape the August calendar page on her little table so she can know what month it is. That I can do. That I can do.

Jenny, my mother's roommate, wheels into the room and smiles as I am taping up the new month my mother has to live through. She seems to want to chat. She can't chat, she's stone deaf. She wants to visit; she doesn't know what she's walked in on.

My mother is finished with her outburst, though. She says to me, "Do you two have grocery shopping to do?"

"No—but we're going to buy a light for over the bathroom sink."

"Then you should get going," she says. "Before it gets too late."

J. stands up. He knows we should take our cue and not wait for another act.

"Merrill," my mother says. "How long have I been here in this place?"

"Two years, two months," I tell her.

I can see her counting the weeks, the days, the hours, the seconds contained in that length of time. The milliseconds she has been shackled to that bed.

"Don't feel guilty that you were upset," I whisper to her before I leave. "It's normal to need to vent your feelings. Don't feel bad about it."

But as I walk with J. out the front door and into the hellish heat, I wonder what to do with how bad *I* feel.

∾

In the lamp store, we look at lamps, we look at chandeliers, we look at Casablanca fans. Someone buys a fifteen-foot-high crystal chandelier and has it loaded by some workmen into his truck outside. The crystals look like cheap glass, they clank against one another, they do not ring like tinkling bells.

J. and I look at all varieties of over-the-sink lights, fluorescent bands, halogen flares, little glowing tulips, flying swans with flashing tail feathers. What is the point? All I will see illuminated in the bathroom mirror is myself getting older and older. I will melt into an ancient crone in a matter of minutes and be strapped to my bed in a nursing home. I don't want to live that way.

"J.," I whisper. "If you are alive by the time I am trapped like my mother, and, if I ask you, will you bring me my sleeping pills?"

"There's no reason to talk about it now," he says.

"Yes, there is!" I insist. "I may not be *able* to talk about it then. I'll probably be locked inside my head, unable to talk or move. So I'm asking you now."

We are standing under a great bronze lamp whose light shines upon us as if we are on a stage.

"Don't worry," my husband says. "We're not going to waste one good minute worrying about it now."

"Would you call this one of the good minutes?" I ask my husband.

∾

J. takes me out to dinner at an Italian restaurant. I eat something called *Panzotti De Formaggi* with carbonara sauce. I drink a whole glass of wine. I eat a chili pepper from my salad. Arias from Italian operas are played over the loudspeakers. I notice people at other tables laughing, toasting one another. The women's earrings sparkle in the light of the little candles burning on the tables. No one seems to be aware that the nursing home is waiting for each one of them. No one seems to have any inkling that gourmet Italian food does not come in feeding tubes. Or that such things as shower chairs and call cords will be their fate. Why don't they know? *I* know! I seem to know nothing else.

∾

In the middle of the night, I awaken in panic. My heart is pounding, I'm soaked with sweat. I leave J.'s side, getting out of bed very quietly. I go into the kitchen, where I make myself some tea and turn on the television set. Something is really wrong with me.

I don't know what it is till it's imminent—I have to throw up. I barely get to the bathroom in time. And I do throw up, again and again, all night—I am turned inside out. I'm violently ill, both diarrhea and vomiting, shaken by spasms of such strength that I'm astonished. I'm flung about till I'm shivering, with only a few minutes of respite between attacks. I don't even inhabit this body—some monster is in there, taking it over.

J. appears in the bathroom doorway, alarmed, looking for me. But I'm not there—I wave him away, meaning *Later, I'll be with you soon, I'm taken for now. I'm possessed!*

At a certain point in the night, seeing my haggard face in the mirror, I think, *How much longer can I stand this?* and then I realize it's only been going on a few hours. Just a few hours of discomfort and I'm desperate! My mother has been in that one bed for two years, two months: how many hours is that? That's 790 days, at 24 hours a day, that's . . .

I stagger to my desk and get my calculator. I have to hold it under the desk lamp to activate the solar power: I hold off the retching that is beginning in my gut and do my arithmetic. The answer is: 18,960 hours. The answer is: 1,137,600 minutes. In seconds that would be . . .

~

When dawn arrives, I am sitting up, wrapped in a comforter on the couch, waiting for the sun to rise. The tension that comes with pain is subsiding gradually. I can feel my insides falling back into place. As the second hand of the wall clock clicks on its path, I can sense, in ticking certainty, the oppressive pressure letting up, fading away. I have, for the first time since last night, a belief that I will actually live. Whatever this was—food poisoning, an allergy to an overdose of mortality—it's over.

I'm going to live. There's a future ahead. I am so grateful I could fall to my knees. Weak and limp, I creep back into bed and take J.'s hand. His fingers, squeezing mine, are warm. Exhausted, I give myself up to the unnegotiable terms of life, and to sleep, without another thought.

August 5

A t least my mother has lived to hear good news. Her granddaughter, my daughter Joanna, has called us to announce her
coming marriage to the young man she brought home to meet us
during the summer. I arm myself with this news, as well as with a
small lamp that I hope my mother can turn on and off with the tiniest pressure of just one finger; I tread with more fear than usual into
the nursing home.

I see that Jenny's daughter is also visiting. I hope this will bode
well for my mother's self-control. I don't feel as if I could tolerate
another scene just now; I don't know if I would feel as sympathetic
as I did a few days ago. Since my mother's last outburst, I have found
myself thinking about my own feelings, and noticing my state of
mind moving from empathy and pity to a state of resentment: how
could she have done that to me, how could she have put me through
that? I am just not up to it again.

After all, my mother has been in this state, more or less, for two
years and two months. Do we—each time I visit—have to redefine
the story, proclaim its horror and unfairness? Do we have to do it
every time?

Jenny and her daughter are not sharing histrionics, I can see that.
They are talking softly (as softly as one can talk to Jenny, who is
deaf), and exchanging news.

As I come into the room, Jenny says to me, "Your mother has had a very bad day," and her daughter shushes her. She says, "Let Jessie tell it herself."

"What?" my mother says, always alert. "What did she say?"

"She said you had a bad day."

"A bad day," she says. "What other kind is there?"

And off we go. Today's complaint is that her aide would not put her back in bed. The aide told her she's too fat, that she weighs too much, that she can't be lifted by one person, and there aren't two available to lift her. So my mother was made to sit up in the wheelchair for six hours, till she was exhausted.

I sigh at the irony. A year ago my mother didn't weigh eighty pounds. Now that she is on the feeding tube which pumps fluid into her at a steady, grinding rate, she has blown up like a balloon.

"I'll talk to the director," I tell my mother. "I'll talk to the charge nurse. I'll talk to the administrator. I'll . . ."

"Oh, what's the use of talking?" my mother says. "Why not just die?"

What do I say to that? That I'm tired of hearing all this talk about dying?

My mother adds, "I've been thinking, what could I possibly die of? My heart is good. What else can go wrong? I have no idea how I will die."

"Let's not talk about dying so much, Ma," I say. "I'm tired of it."

And she closes her mouth. I realize I should have said this long ago. Just: "That's enough. I won't listen to this."

I am seeing my mother suddenly as someone who is abusing me, abusing my patience, my kindness, my love.

I tell her about Joanna's engagement. She will be married in the spring. My mother smiles, and tears come to her eyes. What are these tears about? I don't want to know. I don't want to hear: *I hope I don't live to the wedding.* I don't want to hear: *I'll never be able to go to the wedding.* I don't want to hear whatever it is that turns all the attention back upon her. How sad, how sick, how useless, how helpless she is. I realize I am terribly angry! I want something else from her, I want my mother back!

And my mother says, "I hope they'll be happy together."

All right. Now tears come to *my* eyes. I love her all over again; I'm sorry to have thought these thoughts. She is my mother. She does have a heart.

I notice that Jenny's daughter is leaving; with a brisk wave to her mother in the wheelchair, and one to me and my mother, she's out the door. No operatic farewells, no arias of grief. Jenny, who is ninety-two, and who only gets a visit once a week, sits there like a good soldier, smiling after her daughter's form disappears down the hall.

But I—I pull up a chair and sit down for a long visit. I can't get off that easy. I need to put in my time. I pull out the little lamp, and prepare to argue with my mother, who will say she can't handle it, can't handle anything. After all, this is what I do with my mother. This is the content of our life together.

August 12

J. and I are half-asleep in the sluggish quiet of end-of-summer. We are restless, but feel uninspired and lazy. We would like to go somewhere, but only if someone handed us tickets, an itinerary, and a large cash prize. We want adventure and new experiences, but we don't want to leave the comfort of our bed, our kitchen, our conveniences. Besides, we can't. I have my mother to take care of, and Maxie, too.

J. has installed various games on both our computers, and we guiltily sit for hours, in separate rooms, playing electronic blackjack, solitaire, word games, even golf. Maxie often sits in my lap, watching the arrow of my "mouse" fly across the computer screen. He, too, by his standards, is listless, wilted by the heat, and doesn't even feint at the moving dot with a paw.

My sister stops in to visit. She remarks on our antisocial behavior, saying that if we're going to play blackjack, we might as well do it "for real" and do it with other human beings.

I dare her to come with us on a trip to Las Vegas; within two minutes (unknown to J.) we are poring over the Sunday ads for various hotels and casinos until we find a bargain—not in Las Vegas, but in Laughlin, Nevada, which is situated on the Colorado River about 270 miles from here.

"Twenty-four dollars a night for a room!" she says. "Plus breakfast and a show starring an imitation Michael Jackson. How can we *not* go?"

"How *can* we go?" I say. "What about Mother? What about Maxie?"

"They'll be fine. My son will feed the cats; Mom will be okay. We could go for just a night or two."

I can feel my blood stirring; yes, it would be good to take a ride, see something new, have a sense of adventure, maybe hear jackpot bells ringing.

"I'll tell J. our plan," I say. "If he agrees, we have a deal."

~

By dawn the next morning, we three are ready to leave. The cooler is packed with ice for the trip across the desert, J. and I have counted out our disposable money (or so we think), my sister has arranged for her son to feed Maxie and Big Kitty. We are all in excellent spirits; our blood is up, a challenge is in the offing.

I consider stopping off at the nursing home to say good-bye to my mother—but I decide to spare myself the explanations, the justifications, the rationalizations. I just want to go. To fly away. To have a vacation. To pack up my troubles in my old kit bag, and smile, smile, smile. (Besides, in the past, knowingly or not, my mother has managed to create more than one emergency on the eves of such events.)

~

The casino is cold despite the fact that outside the temperature registers 112 degrees. The virtue of gambling is that the act requires you to forget your troubles, and that includes the vagaries of the natural world. So intent am I on my rolls of nickels, and the blessed quality of my particular slot machine, that I hardly remember I have a life in the real world. What matters is: will three sevens appear on the payoff line? Will the Wild Joker line up and double my jackpot? Should I pace myself and put in one nickel at a time or go for it and play three coins at a shot? The decisions are serious and important; they take all my energy. It is here that I will find out whether or not

I have "luck." It is here that I will learn if life will smile upon me. I am vaguely aware that J. is somewhere in the hopeful masses, playing blackjack, and my sister is working away in another row of slot machines, testing how the universe will treat her. I sink gratefully into the noisy dream of clanging bells, raucous shouts, and the eternal hope of winning.

~

Good, having upped the stakes, I hear a siren go off and see I have won 320 quarters! Hours may have passed, or minutes. I can't be sure. Am I tired? Am I hungry? It doesn't matter: I am *lucky*. I feel fired up with hope. The coins sit hot in the metal bowl, promising hours ahead of excitement and possibility.

~

Much later, I convene with J. and my sister. We have had luck, we have lost luck, we are busy counting our money. We persuade one another to take time off for a sandwich. We can hardly sit still in the pounding energy of the walls around us.

After we eat, after it is dark, with the temperature down to perhaps a hundred degrees, we walk along the river front to the next casino. The hotel is in the shape of a great riverboat, with a paddle wheel and a flashing sign that says "Colorado Belle." We agree to play there awhile, meet at an appointed time, and travel on to another casino on the river.

Somewhere in the midnight hours, I find myself exhausted, in the casino of a hotel whose name I don't even know; I sink down on a stool in front of an electronic poker game and notice that I am staring out an enormous glass window at the black waters of the Colorado River. Reflected in the glass is the panorama of gambling souls in the vast room behind me. What I see is a vision of all of humanity gathered together in a common fate, each person bent over a hand of cards, or peering intently at the display of spinning reels and wheels, each person sinking slowly into the swirling waters of the river.

It's a trick of light, of reflection, but every gambler is waist deep in river water, unaware, impervious to the cold and the current, sinking deeper at every moment.

I stare transfixed. This is a vision I couldn't have imagined, guessed at, dreamed in my wildest dream. This—I decide—is why I was drawn to leave my comfortable house, in order to confront this moment.

I, too, am one of the many sinking in the waters of the river. It's rather pleasant, actually—all of us, calmly playing our hands, agreeably accepting our fate, chatting to those on either side of us, as we play and sink.

I gather up my heavy plastic cup of coins and find a machine. I drop in three quarters. I hear the whirr of reels. I listen for the trumpet call, the cascade of silver. Not hearing it, I straighten my shoulders . . . and begin again. This is merely the nature of life.

~

On the trip home across the desert, the three of us recount our adventures to one another. At one point, my sister tells us, she almost won a giant jackpot . . . but had forgotten to put in the third and necessary coin. J. tells us about the man at his table who bet five hundred dollars on each hand of cards. I tell them about the woman who sat beside me and admitted, "I always know I'm going to lose, so why do you suppose I play anyway? I always come here—I love this."

We are animated, energized by our confrontation with fate in the desert. (We have all lost our money.)

My sister asks me if I remember the time we took our mother to Las Vegas. My mother took care of our children, going with them to the game arcade while J. and I wandered through the casino of The Sahara. She reminds me of the photo of my mother, her arm hooked over the neck of a plaster camel in front of the hotel, my three daughters arranged around her.

My mother! Which mother? I have almost forgotten her! I try to pull her image into my mind; my mother and a camel. My mother playing a pinball game. But no, that was a different mother, living another life. Do I have a mother now? What is she to me? I try to summon up an image of her and superimpose it over the passing landscape of twisted Joshua trees and mountains of sand. What comes to me is a mirage of a woman imprisoned and paralyzed in a hospital bed. She must have had a bad hand dealt to her. An unlucky pull on the one-armed bandit's handle. The reels keep spinning. Nothing lines up. There is no winning this one. *I'm so sorry, Mother.* I close my eyes, and let J. drive us safely across the desert.

September 4

Maxie sleeps on the roof of the house at night. When I go out to get the paper at dawn, I hear the creaking of the roof shingles. His little head appears above me, hanging over the edge, his face upside-down to me, mine upside-down to him. He cries to me, extends a paw as if he wishes me to reach up and lift him down.

"Sorry, Maxie, you'll have to find a way down yourself," I say, and walk out to the curb to retrieve the newspaper. By the time I have regained the front steps, he is on *terra firma*, apparently annoyed that he had to traverse the roof, find the tree, make his way down. He's cranky from the effort and nips at my ankles to signal he wants his breakfast, *and right now.*

I don't know where he learned this technique, this sharp-pronged demand, this partly aggressive and partly petulant complaint, suggesting I haven't considered how urgently he wants to eat, and how soon. (I suspect Kitty has schooled him in this lesson, Kitty, whose only raison d'être is food.)

There's an army of yellow jackets waiting for the same food Maxie waits for. The instant I place Maxie's dish on the step, two or three of these insects dive-bomb to the meat and hang there, hovering, buzzing, trying to push their way into the delicacy. Maxie doggedly keeps eating, but Kitty is either too scrupulous to share his meal with other mouths, or he fears getting stung. He backs away, and within five minutes the bowl is not only populated with buzzing yellow jackets, but is also filled with millions of ants—he can't even approach it.

I have tried feeding both cats in the house—which defeats the yellow jackets, but not the ants. (I then have to get the ants out of my kitchen.)

So I take the tack of rotation, choosing a different uninfested outdoor place to feed the cats, sometimes by the back door, sometimes by the front door, and sometimes—for Kitty alone since Maxie won't go near this place—at the pool deck.

~

The hiding place where I first discovered Maxie, in the crawl space under the house near the pool, seems, even now, to terrify him. Likewise, the surrounding area of the pool seems to create a sense of panic in him. Sometimes, before I swim, I take him out and sit on a chair, holding him in my lap, but he fears the noise of the filter motor, he hates the look of the water. As soon as I release my grip, he's leapt up on the pool wall, and gone over!

Do kittens have primal memories? Does Maxie really associate that area of the house with being lost, hungry, cold, frightened?

~

Our love affair has matured. We don't yearn toward one another as much as we did. He isn't as adorable, isn't as inventive, curious, mischievous, isn't as "new." And he must regard me the same way—he knows the limits of our shared ecstasy—knows just how long he can occupy my lap (before we both get tired and wish to go on to something else), knows exactly the nature of the food I will offer him (he likes French toast, fried matzo, anything with egg or cheese, but hates boiled corned beef, meat flavored with soy sauce or garlic, and really despises canned tuna fish, though he will eat any part of a piece of grilled salmon—bones, skin, and all).

We are beginning to know one another as an old married couple might; I know the places on his body he enjoys having touched, and know the sensitive areas he wants me to keep away from. He knows how to test my limits; he will leap upon my bed, sink onto my down comforter, insinuate himself onto my pillow, but when he crawls under the covers, I draw the line. J. is not anxious to share our bed with fleas. Maxie knows he is not my only love; he recognizes that he must share me with J., but he makes it clear that I must also share him with the call of the wild. There's always the moment when he's lounging sleepily against me that his ears prick up, that he senses some urgency I don't perceive, a call to which he must respond. He seems to fly at those moments—there's an arc of movement, my lap lightens, he's gone! I am left with a sense of profound emptiness.

Yet even as he grows away from me, there is something sublime about how Maxie connects me to life, to love, to nature, to history, to the future, to my own animal existence, to a higher awareness of beauty, to a sense of peace, to eternity. His acceptance of his own alive state—his appreciation of "the moment" without fear, anticipation, or worry—is a lesson I take to heart.

I am aware more than ever that change is rule, constancy an illusion. Situations that seem static (and sometimes feel endless) are changing shape insidiously, irrevocably. Maxie was my baby for a time, I was my mother's. Like the folds of an accordion making beautiful music, we have come together and must be pulled apart. Without change, there is no music, there is no dance.

One day I will get a call from the nursing home, and the news they give me will transform my mother from an obligation to a memory. One day perhaps Maxie will come to me (as Big Kitty does) mainly for the bowl of food in my hand.

In the meantime, we do what is required. We live in the moment.

September 5

My sister tells me that our mother wishes to go back to the Bible Study activity because the born-again preacher is more interesting than nothing. She says he has energy. She says he gives interesting arguments for the existence of eternal life.

I wonder if my mother could wish to be saved; I wonder if a crack could occur in the shell of her cynicism. I wonder if any of us, when old, when near the end, could begin to consider certain systems of thought that provide some comfort, that talk of life after death.

When I visit her today, I hear her voice as I walk down the hall. I assume she is talking to someone, perhaps has a visitor. She sounds animated, her voice is strong. But as I draw closer, I hear the words she is saying, that screenplay which has only one line, the script of her life condensed to one hard pellet of need: "I wish I were dead. I wish I were dead."

"What is it, Ma?" I say, hurrying into the room.

"I was abandoned," she says. "After the Bible Study class, they left me there, in limbo." Her face is pale, she is sunken in her bed, the feeding tube spinning its arrow beside her, her head pushed forward by too many pillows. "After the activity, the aides took everyone back to their rooms for lunch—but since I don't have to eat, they left me there. There was no one in the room. They didn't come back for me. They forgot me. After an hour, I started screaming, 'Someone help me! Nurse, please, help me.' No one came. I was afraid. No one passed by. Everyone was eating lunch. I thought they would never find me. That I would be there alone all night in the dark. That I would die there."

My mother's expression is fierce, as if she is thinking, *What else could I expect? This is my fate!* My heart sinks, imagining her there in that room, alone and afraid, with me nowhere in sight. (Where was I at that moment? Happily watering my hanging plants? Holding Maxie in my lap out in the sunshine of the patio?)

"You know they would have found you eventually," I tell her.

"How do I know? How do *you* know?" my mother says to me, her eyes dark as coals.

"Well, they did find you, didn't they?"

"Not before I screamed and begged for someone to come. Not before I got hoarse shouting for help."

"I'm sorry, Mom," I say. "I'm sorry. I'm so sorry. I'm sorry you have to live this way. I'm sorry the world works this way. I'm sorry you're old. I'm sorry you don't live with me. Ma, do you *want* to live with me? Do you want me to take you home and try to take care of you there?"

I mean it, desperately and absolutely. Tears are spilling out of my eyes. My guilt burns me. I am being consumed in the flames of guilt as I picture my mother wild-eyed in a wheelchair, calling for help, and no one hearing her. *Where am I that I do not hear her!*

I reach blindly for a handkerchief. My mother is looking at me with deep concern. For the first time in all these months, in these two years that she has been here, in all the hours that I have come here and sat at her side, I feel her *looking at me.*

"Darling," she says. "I need the care I get here. I get good care here. I have medical attention twenty-four hours a day. They give me what I need."

"Do they, Ma?" I say, wiping my eyes with my handkerchief. "*Do* they take care of you? They leave you alone in a room for hours! They forget you!"

"They do the best they can. But they couldn't forget me for long. Someone would have found me. Someone did. Don't cry, Merrill."

My mother extends her good hand toward me, shakily. I take it in mine, feeling the soft skin, the thinness of her flesh. She—for the first time in all this time—is comforting *me*. I feel myself fold in the swoon of needing her, in the desperate need to be taken care of by my mother. I bow my head and cry in earnest, my shoulders shaking. I cry for her pain, and for my own. I cry for the grief of sickness and old age. I cry for the way the world has to be.

My mother indicates that I should come to her. I lower the bed rails and bend over her, bowing my face to her face. My mother, who has only a few times in her life kissed me earnestly and from her heart, lifts her face up to kiss me now. She kisses my eyes, she presses her forehead to mine.

"Don't cry, darling. I was lost, but now I'm found. *You* found me."

We look long and hard into each other's faces, our eyes locked, till the white figure of the nurse appears with my mother's portion of pain relief.